John and Pat Underwood

walk & eat around
AVIGNON

CONTENTS

This pocket guide is designed for short break walking holidays based on Avignon, at the apex of what we call the 'golden triangle', with the Roman cities of Nîmes and Arles forming the base. Both Avignon and Nîmes are served by TGV and discount airlines, Avignon by daily coach and Eurostar from May to September. The walks can be reached by public transport (or by car), and the climate makes for brilliant walking — and eating — all year round.

Hop on a train, plane or bus for a long weekend or a week. This guide has enough walks, excursions, restaurants and recipes to last almost two weeks — so you can pick and choose the most appealing. The highlights at a glance:

- 10 varied day walks, each with city plan or topographical map
- recommended restaurants
- recipes to make at your self-catering base or back home
- hints on wheat-, gluten- and dairy-free eating and cooking in Provence

INTRO

THE WALKS

The walks range from strolls around the three great cities of Avignon, Nîmes and Arles to some undemanding walks in the Alpilles and at the edge of the Lubéron. The book is specifically designed for visitors using public transport. If you've only a long weekend, you may not want to spend time filling in forms to hire a car. Of course, if you *do* want to hire a car, you will have many more options. Our wider-ranging book, *Landscapes of Western Provence* (see www.sunflowerbooks.co.uk), would take you from Aix-en-Provence to the Pyrenees via 12 car tours and 36 walks.

But rest assured that you do not need your own wheels to discover the glory of the 'golden triangle'. All the walks in this book are easily reached by bus or train, and getting to the walks is half the fun. Sightsee while someone else does the driving. It's amazing how much ground you can cover in just a week.

THE RESTAURANTS

There are restaurants at the start and end of all the walks; in the cities they are everywhere. But, apart from those in the cities, some of them close out of season — just when the walking is at its best! We have concentrated on restaurants that are open all year round and, in the three cities, those that are at the 'heart of the action', *not* the *recherché* places on back streets. The reason is twofold: if it is your first visit, we think you will want to soak up the atmosphere in the main squares; secondly, *out of season*, the 'hidden away' restaurants may be almost empty (most disheartening) — or *closed*. Note that restaurants are generally

Following our Avignon walk, you'll pass this restaurant, called 'Tarasque' on Rue des Teinturiers. It was closed, but we were enchanted by the sign above the door (which lights up at night). Several churches in Provence have paintings about this legend — wherein St Martha, making the sign of the Cross, tamed and captured the Tarasque, a dragon-like monster which periodically emerged from the Rhône to devour anyone in its way.

open for lunch from 12.00-14.00 and for dinner from 19.00-21.00 or 22.00. *No restaurant has paid, in cash or in kind, to be included in this guide.*

THE RECIPES

Most of our recommended restaurants were happy to share with us the *ingredients* used in their recipes, but the actual preparation remains their 'secret' (in truth, they are simply not written down, but just passed on from cook to cook over the years). So you can rest assured that we have cooked *all* of these recipes ourselves, to make sure they 'work'!

What we cannot guarantee, of course, is that they will taste as good back home as they did in France! So many factors come into play to make food taste better when you are in Provence — from the intangibles (the relaxed atmosphere) to the tangibles (the marvellous variety of super-fresh produce you can seek out at the markets).

So if you are in self-catering, why not try some of these recipes while you're still there? We've made most of these dishes on the simple kind of cooker usually found in self-catering (two rings and a decent oven). Many of them are casserole-style, not only easily managed with limited cooking facilities, *but* also virtually impossible to overcook, and there is hardly any washing-up! What's more, they always taste better when reheated after a few days. And good news for anyone suffering food intolerances: all of the recipes can be **gluten- and dairy-free** (see page 138).

PLANNING YOUR VISIT
When to go

The simple answer is — anytime, but remember that from **mid-June to mid-September** it's usually swelteringly hot, crowded to overflowing, and prices are at their highest. Moreover, some of the countryside walks will be closed; see 'Fire hazard' on page 72. On the other hand, most of the excursions suggested on pages 20-23 and some bus services *only* operate in summer, more restaurants open … and the lavender is in full bloom…

Despite the reduced facilities outside summer, that's when we prefer to visit. **Late September and October** are ideal for the mild temperatures and the autumnal colours. One has to take a chance with possibly heave rains in October and **November**, but you can still expect temperatures in the 60s (17-19°C).

We often go at **Christmas/New Year**, to enjoy the festivities

Place de l'Horloge in January — the carousel (in front of the theatre) is just being cleaned before opening for business.

and the clear winter skies. The early mornings can be nippy, but once the sun is up it's fine and warm — *super* walking weather. And unless it is unseasonably cold (below the mid-40s — 7-8°C) or a *mistral* is blowing, the terraces in front of the cafés will be full of people eating out of doors.

February is warmer still, and by **March** it's virtually spring. Plan on some rainy days in March and **April**, but rainy spells don't usually last very long. And at least when it rains here, there's plenty to do indoors (apart from trying new recipes).

May and early June, with wild flowers galore, are simply glorious, as you would expect. And that's when Eurostar starts running direct from London 3-4 times a week!

Where to stay

Of course there is a wide choice of hotels of all grades throughout the area described in this book. While the *best* public transport base is Avignon centre, there are good, fast connections to adjacent Villeneuve-les-Avignon, Nîmes and Arles, as well as frequent buses to St-Rémy.

Rather than an hotel, consider staying in an apart-hotel (some of them have gyms or spas; all have wifi access). Or in someone's city apartment: if you search the web for 'apartment in Avignon' for example, you will be offered hundreds of sites, including many privately-owned second homes. But *beware* (unless you are hiring a car): what is advertised as an apartment in Avignon could be several kilometres outside the centre.

What to take

Remembering that this is to be a carefree week or weekend, pack simply! You don't have to 'dress' for dinner in Provence, no matter how elegant the restaurant.

We manage with a rucksack each, by wearing our walking boots on the flight. Apartments usually have laundry facilities (and there are also many laundries and launderettes in the city centres), so you needn't take a lot of clothing either.

No special equipment is needed for any of the walks, but proper **walking shoes** will help you pound the pavements in the cities. If you plan to walk in the countryside, **walking boots** are preferable to any other footwear, as most walks cross very stony terrain at some stage, and good ankle support is essential. In wet weather you will also be glad of the waterproofing and grip. A **sunhat** and high-protection **suncream** are equally important; there is a real risk of sunstroke on some walks, even outside high summer. Each member of the party should carry a small **rucksack**, so that the chore of lugging the essentials is shared. *All year round* it is advisable to carry a first-aid kit, whistle, torch, spare socks and shoe- or bootlaces, and some warm clothing — as the *mistral* can blow up suddenly, with temperatures dropping as much as 10°C/20°F! A long-sleeved shirt and long trousers should be worn or carried, for sun protection and for making your way through the prickly plants of the *maquis*. Depending on the season, you may also need a windproof, lightweight rainwear, woollies and gloves. Optional items include swimwear, a Swiss Army knife (*don't* pack this in hand luggage, or it will be confiscated), insect repellent, and of course your mobile or smartphone. Mineral water is sold almost everywhere in plastic half-litre bottles (which you can then refill from the tap); outside the towns, where you can stop at bars or cafés, *it is imperative that each walker carries at least a half-litre of water — a full litre or more in hot weather.*

Planning your walks

The walks are specifically designed for access by the excellent **local transport** network … so that you can enjoy a bottle of wine with lunch! Unfortunately, this has meant omitting some of the best countryside walks in the area, in favour of more town walks. But if you *do* want to hire a **car**, you'll be glad to know that all of the routes in this book are easily done from a car.

The walks have been **graded** for the deskbound person who nevertheless keeps reasonably fit. Our timings average 4km per hour on the flat, plus 20 minutes for every 100m/300ft of ascent. None of the walks ascends more than about 350m/1150ft, although there are one or two steep descents. Remember that these are *pure walking times;* increase the overall time by *at least* 50 percent, to allow for any breaks and nature-watching.

Safety depends in great part on *knowing what to expect and being properly equipped.* For this reason we urge you to read through the *whole* walk description at your leisure *before* setting out, so that you have a mental picture of each stage of the route and the landmarks. On *most* of these walks you will encounter other people — an advantage if you get into difficulty. Nevertheless, we advise you not to walk alone in the countryside, especially in winter, when there may be no one else about.

The **plans** for the city walks have been adapted from free tourist board plans; the **maps** for the countryside walks from the latest IGN 1:25,000 maps, which have been reproduced at a scale of 1:35,000 (the relevant IGN map numbers, should you wish to go further afield, are shown in the 'logistics' panel facing each walk introduction).

One of the reasons why walking in France is such a joy is the good **waymarking** and **signposting**.

Basically you will encounter two types of waymarked route in the countryside:

PR (Petite Randonnée) or 'short walk' routes, waymarked in yellow (or sometimes green) and usually signposted;

GR (Grande Randonnée) or 'long-distance' routes, waymarked in red and white, but not *always* signposted.

At the top of each walk we mention the waymarking colours *at time of writing.* Do, however, note these waymarking features, common to both PR and GR routes: = means continue this way, X means do not go this way, ⌈ means turn right and ⌉ turn left.

Free **GPS track** downloads are available for all the countryside walks in this book: see the *Walk & eat around Avignon* page on the Sunflower website. *But even if you don't use GPS*, the maps are accurate enough to enable you to easily compare them with Google Maps on your smartphone and pinpoint your exact position. It's also great fun to open the GPS tracks on Google Earth to preview the walks in advance!

Verifying timetables in advance

While transport details are given in the 'logistics' panel at the start of each walk (with more details and websites on pages 132-133), remember that these timetables were *correct at time of writing*. The *very best* way to verify departures and returns is at the information desk at the **relevant railway or bus stations** (shown on the town plans) after you arrive. But if you want to plot out some walks in advance, you can verify most timetables on-line before you travel.

Trains are operated by TER (Transports Express Régional), part of the SNCF (Société Nationale des Chemins de Fer). You can search most journeys in English at **en.oui.sncf**. *Do look at this site first, in case you don't read French and have to grapple with the French site later.* If you do have to use the French website (**www.ter-sncf.com**), here is an example, based on Walk 2.

- at the home page click on 'Réservez votre billet'
- then scroll down to 'Provence-Alpes-Côte d'Azur'
- a page comes up: 'Horaires et Achats'
- under 'Départ', select 'Gare', then type in Avignon
- if there is more than one station (as in Avignon) you have to be specific: select 'Avignon Centre' from the drop-down menu
- at 'Arrivée', select 'Gare', then type in type in Nîmes

The beautiful ceiling and organ in the church of St-Martin in St-Rémy

- at 'Date d'aller' use the calendar to pick day of travel
- at 'À partir de', use the drop-down menu to choose the departure time
- at 'Date de retour' do the same
- click 'Rechercher'

Five departure times from Avignon come up to view; arrival times and total journey times are also shown. To see *earlier* times, click on 'Horaires précédents' (below left); to see *later* times, click on 'Horaires suivants'.

To see times of return trains, you have to pretend to buy an outgoing ticket first:

- so click on 'Acheter' for the time you would theoretically take the train, then click on 'Choisir cet aller'.

Intercity buses are operated by a plethora of private firms. For each walk, we give you a website and telephone numbers where you can update the bus times shown in the book (see pages 132-133), *but* unless you are a web expert and/or French-speaking, we heartily recommend that you *use the timetables we give as a guide only, then visit the local tourist office or bus station and ask them to confirm the latest routes, departure times and departure points for you.*

City buses are also perplexing because of the multiplicity of operators, although services are good. For **Avignon** you can download *(téléchargez)* a PDF of routes at **www.tcra.fr** (click on 'Plan', then on 'Réseau'), for **Nîmes** at **www.edgard-transport. fr** (click on 'Plans du réseau', then download) and for **Arles** at **www.tout-envia.com** (English site!; under 'Travelling', select 'Network map'). All the operators feature different passes and discounts — 4-day to monthly passes, passes that can also be used on the trains, discounts for families and over 65s, etc. Unless you read French (only the Arles site is in English), again, we advise you to go to the local tourist office and let them work through the maze for you.

Bus stations in the three large cities are located next to the railway stations (see town plans); all of our city walks start at the railway stations, where there is also parking.

Each time you board a bus or train, you must *validate your ticket* — on buses in the machine behind the driver, for trains at the squat yellow machines in the main halls or just before the platforms.

ON ARRIVAL
Rail and bus passes

If you plan to make good use of rail services, then your first stop should be at the **central railway station** ticket office, where you can buy a suitable pass or a discounted booklet of

> Remember that Avignon has **two railway stations** — the TGV station 4km southwest of the centre and the central station just outside the city walls. If you arrive by Eurostar or TGV, there are shuttle buses to the city centre railway station every 15 minutes.

multiple tickets (*carnet*). Pick up any timetables you want at the same time. Then make for the nearby **bus station** and do the same — and ask for a plan of the routes they cover.

Parking in the cities

Should you decide to hire a car, note that all our city walks start at the railway station, and all these have car parks. In **Avignon**, unless you go early on Saturday or Sunday morning, the paid underground car park will be full. If so, just drive 250m west, past the large Grand Hotel Avignon (18 on the plan): on the far side of the hotel is an underground car park with plenty of space. The station car park in **Nîmes** is very large, and you should have no trouble getting in. But again, there is another underground car park just nearby, beneath the Esplanade Charles de Gaulle. **Arles** is a dream — a large, free, open-air car park in front of the station. In **St-Rémy** we recommend the car park at the tourist office (pay and display).

Just in case you are not used to the automatic ticket machines in city car parks, here are a couple of hints. As you drive in, push the red button at the barrier for a ticket *and keep*

CAISSE AUTOMATIQUE

It certainly had us flummoxed! This is the *Caisse* at Nîmes station. In this machine, your ticket goes into the orange slot ('ticket'), the cost is displayed above. To pay by credit card, use the upper central slot and key pad; for bills the lower central slot; for coins the upper right-hand slot. The green button produces a receipt; the red button means cancel. This machine is very different from those at Avignon.

it with you. On returning to the car park, go to one of the machines marked 'Caisse' (in Avignon these are on each floor; in Nîmes there is just one — above the car park, on the left, just as you exit the back of the station. Insert the ticket into *(usually)* the top slot. The screen will show how much you owe (about 10 € for a full day, in which case it is easiest to pay by credit card). Insert your credit card into *same slot* as the ticket, key in your pin, then wait about two minutes for it to process. For a receipt, press 'Reçu'. At the exit, *insert the paid-up ticket* to lift the barrier.

Tourist information

The **tourist offices** (1 on all the plans), could be one of your first ports of call, to find out what's on during your visit and to pick up a **city plan**. Since they are mostly near the railway stations, our walks pass these offices early on. Should you wish to download any information in advance, you can log onto: www.ot-avignon.fr, www.ot-nimes.fr or www.tourisme.ville-arles.fr.

Most of the tourist offices will give you a free '**pass**' entitling you to discounts on city attractions — museums, monuments, boat trips, or guided tours. But it's not necessary to pick up the pass at the tourist office — they all work in the same way: you pay full entry price at the first attraction you visit and will be given the 'pass' there; this entitles you to reductions of from 20-50% on all subsequent visits to members of the scheme. They are good value if you plan to visit at least three attractions.

Abbaye de St-Martial, next to Avignon's tourist office

Shopping for self-catering

Even if you are foregoing the luxury of staying in someone's beautifully equipped 'second home' (see 'Where to stay', page 8), apartments should have, as a minimum, good-quality kitchenettes with small fridges, two-ring electric burners and, more importantly, quite a good-sized oven. There should be ample crockery, cutlery and cooking utensils, but you may want to pick up a few extra things, like a vegetable peeler and whisk.

Although more exotic shopping trips will come later, make your first port of call the nearest **supermarket,** to stock up on essentials. The main supermarket chain in the city centres is Monoprix, and all are near the walks. In **Avignon** you pass a branch at 24 Rue de la République (19 on the plan; open Mon-Sat, 09.00-19.00); in **Nîmes** it's south of the Porte d'Auguste at 3 Boulevard Amiral Courbet (9 on the plan; open Mon-Sat, 08.30-20.00 and Sun from 09.00-12.00); in **Arles** it's just at the start of the walk at Place Lamartine (21 on the plan; Mon-Sat, 08.30-20.00 *in summer*; Mon-Thu, 08.30-19.30 and Sat from 08.30-20.00 *in winter*).

The supermarkets also have delicatessens, butchers and fishmongers, and this is an easy option if you're shopping in the afternoon, when the local markets aren't usually open.

Markets

Once the staples are in the cupboard, the real shopping fun can begin. In **Avignon** make for **Les Halles** at Place Pie (20 on the plan) — a real Provençal market with 40 stalls under cover selling local produce — open from 06.00 until 13.30 daily except Mondays.

Nîmes also has a covered market called **Les Halles**, linked to a large commercial centre called La Coupole, off Rue Général Perrier (10 on the plan). The opening hours

Supermarket shopping
list reminder
washing-up liquid or
dishwasher tablets
paper towels
aluminium foil
soap
tissues/toilet paper
scouring pads
salt & pepper
mineral water
milk/cream*
coffee/tea/drinking
chocolate
butter*
sugar
bread*
juice
wine/beer/cider
olive oil & vinegar
eggs
tomato purée
rice
mayonnaise/mustard
torch batteries?
vegetable peeler?
whisk?

*see also panel on
page 137 for gf, df
supermarket products

here are very generous — daily, including holidays, from 07.00 till 13.30.

Arles specialises in an outdoor market — 2km long, one of the largest in France, with 1400 merchants selling everything under the sun — it's held on Saturdays along the **Boulevard des Lices**, one of the focal points

At Christmas (and some other festivals) many 'one-man bands' set out stalls at Place de l'Horloge in Avignon — like this sausage- and cheese-maker from the Pyrenees.

for our city walk. There is also a food market on Wednesdays along Boulevard Emile Combes east of the arena.

EXCURSIONS IN THE AREA

By rail, coach or boat, there is plenty of choice in the 'golden triangle'. Our top all year round excursions by train would be day (or overnight) trips to Aix-en-Provence or Marseille. By coach, top of the list would be the Camargue, but there are many other destinations. Year-round boat trips are more limited, but there are a few possibilities. Note that while there are many operators who will take you *privately* (whether by mini-bus, plane, on horseback or in a kayak!), **Avignon** and **Arles** are the best bases for scheduled (less expensive) trips.

Below are some suggestions you might enjoy, but note that some only operate in the summer. The local tourist offices will help you plan seasonal trips to suit your budget and interests.

Excursions by train

Unfortunately the last tourist train in this area (the Petit Train des Alpilles) closed in 2013. The nearest venue for enthusiasts is about 50km to the west: the **Train à vapeur des Cévennes**, a steam railway between Anduze and St-Jean-du-Gard (access: train from Nîmes to Alès, then bus line 72 or 81 to Anduze or bus line A12 from Nîmes to St-Jean-du-Gard).

A longer trip would take you from Nîmes into the Cévennes on **Le Cévenol**: a supremely scenic route through gorges and over viaducts. You need not go all the way to Clermont Ferrand (five hours); day trips are possible. See **les.cevennes.free.fr** (website in French), or enquire at the railway station in Nîmes.

Easiest of all would be a train to **L'Isle-sur-la-Sorgue** (40min

Water wheel in l'Isle-sur-la-Sorgue

from Avignon, 1h 30min from Nîmes or Arles). The town is delightful in itself, with its tree-lined avenues, the teal-blue Sorgue and lovely old waterwheels. There are many restaurants by the river: two favourites are Le Potager de Louise and L'Ecailler. But it's also just a short bus ride to the famous **Fontaine-de-Vaucluse**, the spring where Petrarch sought peace of mind and inspiration — at its gushing best in winter and spring.

Excursions by minibus

Provence Reservation (21 on the plan of **Avignon**) offers **scheduled excursions** in 8-seater minibuses all year round. These may be themed **tours** (lavender fields, vineyards) or trips to famous sights (Pont du Gard, Fontaine de Vaucluse, Camargue, Les Baux). Half-day trips cost around 45-55 € (minimum two people). They also offer **tailor-made trips** but, basically, they will take you virtually anywhere you might like to go. They even organise full holidays. For more information (or a quotation), log on to www.provencereservation.com or

excursions

Year round there are boat trips across the Rhône to Villeneuve (shown above), as well as Arles and Châteauneuf du Pape.

(04 90 14 70 00. Of course there are many more excursion companies in Avignon, Arles and Nîmes, but since Walk 1 takes you right past their door (just before you get to the Pont d'Avignon), it's a good opportunity to see what's on offer.

Excursions by boat

Avignon is the best centre for short cruises on the Rhône. Run by **Les Grands Bateaux de Provence** (www.mireio. net; (04 90 85 62 25), these start from the quay at Allées de l'Oulle (just south of 22 on the Avignon plan). The excursions vary from an hour's trip just viewing the city monuments (about 7.50 €) or a two-hour trip (including a 12-level lock change), to luncheon cruises and dinner dances. The good news is that these operate *all year round,* except when unavoidably curtailed by bad weather or locks closed for maintenance. See the website for pictures of the boats and more details of the cruises.

The **Arles** tourist office website offers a cornucopia of more adventurous trips in the Rhône Delta — botanical and ornithological safaris in kayaks or rubber dinghies, priced from about 35 € up. These generally run from 1/4 until 30/9. For more information (and pamphlets to download), go to www. arlestourisme.com (English pages).

Just two and a half hours from Paris by TGV — six hours from London on Saturdays in summer (when the Theatre Festival is on) — Avignon is an ideal short break destination. Not only is there plenty to see in the city itself, but the fine Roman remains at Nîmes and Arles are just half an hour away.

around avignon

WALK

Start out at the **main railway station** [2]: walk straight ahead through the city walls via the **Porte de la République**. Follow **Cours Jean Jaurès** for 200m/yds, to where the 14th-century **Abbaye de St-Martial** rises on the right. The **tourist office** [1] is just beyond it, also on your right. Call in and stock up on the city plan, brochures about excursions, and calendar of events. You can collect an 'Avignon Pass' here as well — it's free (see page 17).

Out of the tourist office, turn right and right again on narrow **Rue Henri Fabre**, hugging the side of the abbey. A lovely square, **Square Agricol Perdiquier**, lies just beside it. Rue Fabre quickly becomes **Rue des Lices**, a scruffy street initially, which traces the wall of the 13th-century fortifications (*lice* originally referred to wooden

See plan inside front cover

Distance: about 7km/4.3mi; all day

Grade: easy (but tiring nonetheless)

Equipment: see page 9

Transport: 🚋 to Gare Avignon Centre (*not the Gare TGV!*) or 🚌 to the *gare routière* (main bus station) in Avignon — adjacent to the railway station. Or 🚗: park at the railway station (see notes on page 15).

Refreshments: throughout

Market days:
food/general market at Les Halles (daily ex Mon); see page 18
Sat: flower market, Place des Carmes
Sun: flea market, Place des Carmes

Opening times/full entry fee*
Palais des Papes: daily 09.00-19.00, 11 €; Pont St-Bénézet & Ramparts: 09.00-19.00, 5 €; Petit Palais (*cl 1/1, 1/5, 14/7, 1/11, 25/12*): 10.00-13.00 & 14.00-18.00, 6.50 €; Fondation Angladon: Wed-Sun 13.00-18.00, 7 €; Lapidary Museum (*cl Tue, 1/1, 1/5, 25/12*): 10.00-13.00 & 14.00-18.00, 2 €; Calvet Museum (*cl 1/1, 1/5, 25/12*): 10.00-13.00 & 14.00-18.00, 6 €; Requien Museum: Tue-Sat ex holidays, 09.00-12.00 & 14.00-18.00, free entry

*High season opening times; in winter open slightly later and may close for lunch; last visits up to 2 h earlier

The impressive almshouse on Rue des Lices; below: Rue des Teinturiers skirts the Sorgue — a wonderfully evocative street, even in winter

fencing enclosing a strong-hold). Then, on the left, the huge galleried 18th-century **almshouse** [4] takes you completely by surprise. Not far past here, also on the left, is the classical **Chapelle du Verbe Incarné** [5], badly defaced by graffiti.

About 150m further on, at the crossroads, turn right on **Rue des Teinturiers** ('Dyers' Street'), immediately passing a large **belltower** on the right — the remains of a Franciscan convent. This enchanting, plane-shaded, cobbled street runs to the left of the **river Sorgue**, and you will see the reason for the name: the river was used by the cloth-dyers, and several of their large **waterwheels** remain today. But before you come to them you pass to the left of the 16th-century **Chapelle Ste-Croix** (a Grey Penitents' Chapel), restored in the 19th century.

Notice the stone benches alongside the road, obviously fragments from ancient buildings and carved with gargoyles, crosses and even skeins of rope. One of them is dated 1483.

When you come to the town walls, turn back and retrace your steps past Rue des Lices, then take next left turn into **Rue de la Masse**, passing a couple of impressive old mansions. This street becomes **Rue du Roi-René** where, at the corner of Rue Grivolas, you'll find the **Maison du Roi René**: 'Good King René' (under whose reign the region was politically and economically stable, allowing the arts to flourish) supposedly lived here when visiting Avignon from his base in Aix-en-Provence.

You then come into **Place St-Didier**, with its 14th-century eponymous Provençal-style single-nave church [6]. From St-Didier, walk back, around the east end of the church, on **Rue de la Saraillerie**. This runs into a pedestrianised shopping area and takes you straight to **Place de l'Horloge** — the real heart of the city, bustling with cafés and restaurants. The plane-shaded square is named for the 14th-century Gothic **clock tower** *(horloge),* part of the **Hôtel de Ville** [7; Town Hall]. Two large wooden figures, Jaquemart and his wife, strike the hour (but are not easily seen when the trees are in leaf). Next door is the city's **theatre** [8], with a delightful two-tiered **carrousel** in front. A lovely gate on the right fronts the house of Jean Vilar, who founded the Avignon International Theatre Festival. Over the Christmas period, the whole square is 'canopied' with lights, above a large and lively Christmas market with about 20 traders.

Continue north, past the **Banque de France** [9], into the huge **Place du Palais** [10], dominated by the Palais des Papes. (If you

The Mint (Hôtel des Monnaies)

are running out of steam, the 40-minute guided tour of all the sights on the **tourist train** leaves from here.) Before exploring the palace, take time to look at the 17th-century **Hôtel des Monnaies** [**11**; The Mint) on the left, once home of the Borghese family, who administered the city on behalf of the then pope. Later it became the city's mint, and is now the Conservatory of Music. Its baroque façade, with fat cherubs, lions chomping on fruit, and the Borghese coat of arms (dragons and eagles) is in complete contrast to the austerity of the papal fortress.

Despite the fact that the Avignon Papacy only lasted just under 100 years, the city of Avignon remained papal property until 1791 and has always been known as the 'city of the popes'. The massive (15,000 sqm) fortified **Palais des Papes** can be seen from miles around, rising above the city walls. (It consists of two adjacent buildings — the old palace to the north, and the newer one to the south.) Allow a good hour for your visit — either on your own or with a guided tour (in English).

Just north of the palace is the cathedral, **Notre-Dame-des-Doms [12]**. Built in the middle of the 12th century, the cathedral was damaged repeatedly — especially during the Revolution. Most critics are unimpressed by its subsequent rebuilding, citing especially the 1859 addition of a huge gilded statue of the Virgin atop the 15th-century Romanesque bell tower. But whatever the critics say, one cannot help but admit that it is impressive. Inside, the Romanesque dome covering the chancel is remarkable, as is the octagonal lantern over the transept crossing. At Christmas there is a beautiful crib in the cathedral (see page 32).

From the cathedral go through a gate and walk up **Montée des Moulins** to the gardens on the **Rocher des Doms**. From this bluff there is a stupendous view over the curving Rhône and St-Bénézet Bridge, with the Tour Philippe le Bel at Villeneuve behind it. Be sure to go on to the **viewing table**, which will help you identify points much further afield — from the Alpilles to Mont Ventoux.

From the viewing table go back and walk round the shady **duck pond** area (with picnic tables and a seasonal café). Pick your way past the courting couples, heading back towards the cathedral's octagonal lantern. Then retrace your route back down Montée des Moulins. On your right is the **Petit Palais**. This most attractive building was bought by the popes in 1335 and eventually became home to Pope Julius II in the 16th century. A patron of Michelangelo, he took a great interest in the arts and established a fabulous collection of painting and sculptures with two main themes — Avignon in the Middle Ages and early art (the Italian primitives are especially noteworthy). Later the building was often used by the city to house visiting royalty and dignitaries.

Continue back down to the Palais des Papes, then take the

alleyway at the right of the Mint, **Rue de la Monnaie**. This takes you to **Rue de la Balance**, where you turn right. Home to gypsies in the 19th century, the street was completely revamped in the 1970s. Despite some old restored mansions on the right, it's not very attractive, on account of the modern buildings on the left (one of which, No 33, houses Provence Reservation, the minibus tour operator mentioned on page 22). Following brown signposts to 'Pont d'Avignon', go left on **Rue du Puits de la Reille**, right on **Rue de la Grande Fustière** and then left on **Rue Ferruce**. The **Port du Rhône** takes you through the ramparts and out to the famous 'Pont d'Avignon' — **Pont St-Bénézet**. You reach it via a restored **gatehouse** and a '**Musée en Images**' telling the story of the bridge on a huge video screen (English narrative available). *Note that the next part of the walk, along the ramparts, is only possible if you pay to visit the bridge; all other approaches are kept locked.*

The narrow cobbled bridge dates from 1177, built by the 'Bridge Brotherhood' — a group of volunteers inspired by the legend of a young shepherd boy called Bénézet, who had been commanded by an angel to build a bridge at that spot. Standing here, contemplating the full force of the Rhône, it seems astounding that such a project could *ever* have been completed in those days — no less in just 11 years. The original bridge crossed two arms of the river via the Ile de la Barthelasse — 900m/3000ft long, with 22 arches, and ran to the base of Philip the Fair's Tower at Villeneuve. The bridge was rebuilt and raised in the 1230s, at which time a little Gothic-style chapel was superimposed on the Romanesque **Chapelle St-Nicolas**

Pont St-Bénézet: today one has to pay to be 'sur le pont d'Avignon'.

which stands on the centre pier. Today only four of the 22 arches remain — the Rhône finally took its revenge in the floods of 1668, but the setting of this bridge is indescribably lovely.

Return from the chapel and follow the **ramparts** south. These magnificent 14th-century walls still completely encircle the city for a distance of over 4km/2.5mi. Built by order of the popes, the original walls were much higher than they are today (the lower parts now being covered by roads), and there was also a moat outside the walls. Nevertheless, from a military

At Christmas there is a beautiful crib in the cathedral, with huge *santons* — almost half life-size. The tradition goes back to Pope Joan XXII who initiated the custom in the 14th century, but the crib that one sees today is very old as well. Most of the figures and costumes were collected by the Carmelites in the early 19th century; they have since been repaired twice.

standpoint the walls were more symbolic than effective, as they lacked any projecting parapets from which to survey and attack the enemy below.

Only a short section of the ramparts is accessible today, and as you pass the modern road bridge over to Villeneuve, you'll have to descend — into elegant **Place Crillon**, where the famous **Hôtel d'Europe** is on the left (from Napoleon to the present day, anyone who is anyone stays here). Walk across the square and along **Rue Folco-de-Baroncelli**, then go right on **Rue Joseph Vernet**, a posh shopping street (the 'Bond Street' of Avignon). After 150m, opposite a church, turn left on **Rue St-Agricol**. A large staircase leads to the 14th/16th century church of **St-Agricol [14]**, with its finely carved 15th-century façade. Inside there are some noteworthy works of art contemporaneous with the church ... if you're not flagging by now.

Leaving the church, continue on Rue St-Agricol, past the charming courtyard of the **Petit Louvre** hotel on your right; it incorporates the remains of a Knights Templar chapel dating from 1273, now a theatre/conferences venue. Coming to **Rue Bouquerie**, turn right (but first walk left past the east end of St-Agricol, to see some Gallo-Roman rampart ruins behind railings). Walk along Bouquerie, passing under the arch of the **Hôtel du Préfecture [15]** on your left and then past the **Hôtel du Département** facing it. After 200m/yds, turn right on **Rue Horace Vernet**. This brings you back to **Rue Joseph Vernet** — a long street which, like the Rue des Lices near the start of the walk, traces the edge of the 13th-century ramparts. On your right, as you join this street, are two small museums, **Requien** (natural history, botany, zoology), then **Calvet** (with some fine paintings ranging from 16th-century to late 19th). But if you like the Impressionists, perhaps save your 'museuming' for the next, final stop!

Turn left on Rue Joseph Vernet to continue. Coming back to where the tourist office is facing you, you have a chance to see the last Van Gogh painting of Provence still in Provence: walk left on **Rue de la République**, then turn right on **Rue Frédéric Mistral**, by the side of the **Lapidary Museum [16]**, and left on **Rue Laboureur**. At No 5 you will find the **Musée AnglAdon [17]**, set up in the mansion of two great collectors, themselves artists. There are works by Cézanne, Dégas, Modigliani, Picasso, and Van Gogh's *Railway Carriages,* painted in August 1888. Opposite the museum is the **Livrée Ceccano**, a media centre housed in a palace built by a cardinal.

From here retrace your steps to the tourist office and **railway/bus station**.

Le Forum

Location, location, location! We hadn't read any reviews before visiting this restaurant, or we might have stayed away. Some users have deplored its 'touristy' location as well as the mediocre food, saying that there are far better restaurants around Les Halles. But this book is meant for *short break* holidays, and if you've only one day in Avignon then perhaps, like us, you would prefer to

lunch right at the heart of things, facing the town hall, theatre and carousel.

We last visited in winter, joining Avignon's 'ladies who lunch' and businessmen on the warm glassed-in terrace. We chose the very inexpensive *formule* lunch. No sooner had we ordered the *petit salé* shown opposite than a champagne *choucroute* was delivered to the next table; it smelled divine. But we were more than pleased with our choice; maybe we've just been lucky here.

LE FORUM
20 Place de l'Horloge (04 90 82 43 17;
www.leforum-avignon.com (in English)
daily all year 08.00-02.30 €€ (menus at
18.90 € and 26.90 €; 'formule' lunch: dish
of the day and 250 ml glass of wine, 13 €)

large menu, in winter: beef (tartare, grilled, stew, or with *foie gras*); roast rack of lamb with thyme and garlic preserve; duck breast (with sweet-sour sauce or with wild morel mushrooms); grilled pork fillet with chanterelle mushrooms; gambas with garlic and parsley; braised salmon fillet

winter specialities: three *choucroute* (sauerkraut) dishes — with seafood (!), with various Alsatian meats and champagne, with pork knuckle; also *pieds et paquets* (a regional dish of mutton tripe with sheep's feet cooked in white wine)

wide selection of **home-made** cakes and ice creams

restaurants

eat

Petit salé aux lentilles (lean pork belly with lentils)

First draw the salt out of the pork belly: cover it with cold water and leave in the fridge for a good 5 h, changing the water 4-5 times.

Put the pork belly into a cast iron casserole and cover completely with fresh cold water. Add the onion, garlic, bouquet garni and bay leaf — no other seasoning. Bring to the boil, then cook, covered and just lightly bubbling, for about 1 h 30 min. During this time, put the sausages (*unpricked*) in another pan, cover with cold water, and cook gently, *without boiling*, for 30 min. Then let the sausages cool in their own liquid and cut into chunks.

When the pork belly cooking time is up, add the lentils (and carrots) to the casserole. Let this all bubble away *gently* for about 30 min. Then remove the pork, cut into thick slices, and return to the casserole. Discard the onion; add the sausage, and taste. If it's not tangy enough, add a tiny bit of wine vinegar. Serve piping hot, garnished with parsley — with some mustard and a pepper grinder to hand.

Ingredients (for 4 people)

400 g salt-cured lean pork belly (*petit salé* in France)
3-4 sausages of your choice (Le Forum uses traditional fine-grained smoked sausage; we prefer unsmoked)
250 g brown lentils, rinsed
1 small onion, stuck with 1 clove
3 carrots, sliced (optional)
1 bouquet garni
1 bay leaf
1 garlic clove, peeled
wine vinegar (optional)
fresh parsley to garnish
Dijon mustard (to serve)
ground pepper (to serve)

recipes

eat

Nîmes must be one of the most beautiful cities in France; from the moment you leave the 'Romanesque' railway station you walk along elegant squares and boulevards with well-preserved Roman remains. The 18th-century Jardins de la Fontaine, with their exquisite pools and waterways are the icing on the cake!

around nîmes

WALK

The walk starts from the front of **Nîmes Gare** [2]. First look round the station itself — probably the most beautiful railway station you will ever see, with its 'Romanesque arches' and 'catacombs'. As you leave the station, you can see the Tour Magne straight ahead on a hill in the distance — your goal about midway through the walk.

Walk straight ahead on wide **Avenue Feuchères**, then cross the attractive **Esplanade Charles de Gaulle**, where the spire of **Ste-Perpétue** rises to the right. The arena is just ahead to the left; at its right is the **Palais de Justice** [4], fronted by Corinthian columns. You pass the **Fontaine Pradier** (named for the sculptor who designed it): a woman symbolising Nîmes is crowned with a miniature 'Maison Carrée' and surrounded by allegorical figures

Distance: about 5km/3mi; all day

Grade: easy in the lower town, but steps to climb in the arena, an ascent of about 125m/400ft to the Tour Magne, then 150 steps to the top

Equipment: see page 9

Transport: 🚆 to Nîmes Gare or 🚌 to the *gare routière* (bus station). Or 🚗: park at the railway station

Refreshments: throughout

Market days:
food/general market at Les Halles (daily); see page 18

Mon: flower market at the Stade des Costières (the stadium about 3km south of the centre); flea market on Cours Jean Jaurès

Fri: fruit, vegetables, local produce on Cours Jean Jaurès

Opening times/full entry fee*
Arena: daily, 09.00-19.00, 8.50 €**; Maison Carrée: daily, 10.00-19.30, 4.80 €**; Tour Magne: 09.30-19.00, 3 €**; *Museums* (all are open daily ex Mon and 1/1, 1/5, 1/11, 25/12): Contemporary Art, Fine Arts, Bullfighting: all 5.10 €; Archaeological, Natural History, Old Nîmes: all free.

*High season opening times; in winter open slightly later and may close for lunch; last visits up to 2 h earlier

**Joint ticket: these three attractions can be included in one ticket for 11 €

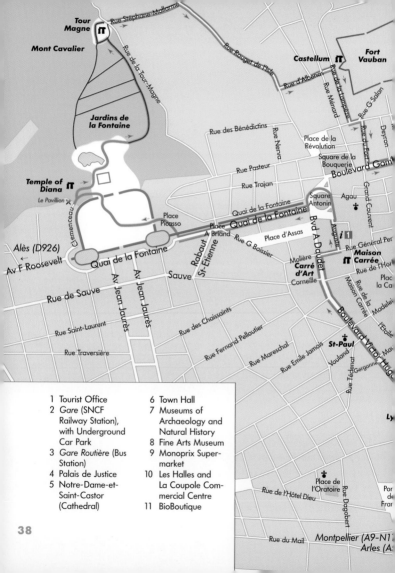

1 Tourist Office
2 *Gare* (SNCF Railway Station), with Underground Car Park
3 *Gare Routière* (Bus Station)
4 Palais de Justice
5 Notre-Dame-et-Saint-Castor (Cathedral)
6 Town Hall
7 Museums of Archaeology and Natural History
8 Fine Arts Museum
9 Monoprix Supermarket
10 Les Halles and La Coupole Commercial Centre
11 BioBoutique

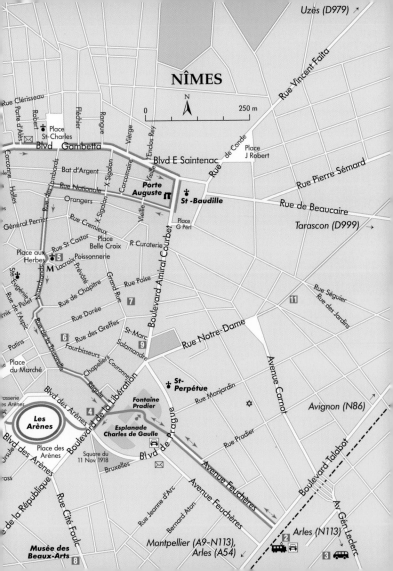

The Romanesque *gare*

representing important water features of the area — including the Gardon and Rhône.

Turn left on **Boulevard de la Libération**, then, almost immediately, go left across **Place des Arènes**, to circle **Les Arènes**, the Roman amphitheatre. Reminiscent of the arena in Arles in size and oval shape, this arena probably dates from the same period (1st century AD). Its dimensions are 133 x 101m (about 450 x 330ft), and it has a capacity of 24,000 spectators. It is one of the best-preserved Roman amphitheatres in existence, where you can still see the delineation of individual seats for the spectators (the holes held poles which supported sheltering awnings).

As you round the outside, the building rises two storeys above you (about 20m/65ft high), with 60 arcades and four entrances. Walk in through the main, northern gateway, decorated with bulls. *(As this will be your first monument visited, pay full entry now — this entities you to a Visitor's Pass and discounts on other attractions in the city.)* Climb to the top-most tiers for a splendid overall view over the 34 tiers of the arena, where spectators were seated according to their social station — patricians in the 'dress circle' and the 'plebs' in the 'upper stalls'. Beneath the arena itself is a maze of vaulted corridors

Les Arènes, with a statue of Christian Montcouquiol ('Nimeño II'), a coura-
geous bullfighter who once defeated six bulls in this arena singlehandedly

and galleries — the 'backstage' area, where gladiators, animals, sportsmen, and chariot drivers all awaited their turn on stage. The lurid posters of today hark back to the original, hand-painted posters of the past, pulling in the crowds by announcing fights to the death in the gory detail. In fact even some executions took place here — for instance, early Christians were thrown to the beasts.

Later, under the influence of Christianity, gladiatorial fights were forbidden (from the early part of the 5th century), and the

On our last visit, the Maison Carrée was in scaffolding for cleaning. At the right is a photograph of the square as it once was, with the old theatre in the background. When asked initially to incorporate the old façade into the new Carré d'Art, Lord Foster refused, on the grounds of cost and artistic integrity.

arena lost its role. The Visigoths rebuilt it as a fortress, which was then taken by the Saracens in the 8th century. By the Middle Ages the inside of the arena had been filled with houses, and by the 18th century about 700 people lived inside its walls, some in conditions of considerable squalour. Only in the 19th century were the buildings demolished and the arena restored. The first bullfight took place in 1853, and bullfights still play an important role in Provençal culture; 'Spanish-style' bullfights are still allowed despite the protests of animal rights activists.

From Les Arènes, start to walk north up **Boulevard Victor Hugo**. On the corner to your right is the Hôtel Brasserie des Arènes, looking most enticing with its huge outdoor terrace — but it's a bit early in the day for lunch! You pass a most attractive *lycée* on the left (with the 'RF' cypher, emblem of the French Republic, below the elegant clock), and then the church of **St-Paul**, also on the left. At this point you will become aware of what looks like a gigantic 'contemporary' white towel rail ahead on the left — the **Carré d'Art**, Lord Foster's incongruous large glass and steel building (1993) which now houses the city library and contemporary art museum (with works from the 1960s to the present). Well, what do *you* think of it? We were shocked, after a decade between visits, to find the whole balance of the square changed. The Nîmois *know* they should be proud of it, but when we got them talking we didn't meet anyone who liked it in this setting; the most optimistic comment was that the view from inside was very fine.

Facing the 'Art Square' is the ancient **Maison Carrée** — what you've really come to see. The 'Square House' is in fact neither a house nor square. It's a beautiful rectangular temple — the very best-preserved Roman temple in the world (in fact, it was just being cleaned during our last visit and was looking splendid). Built in the late 1st century BC, and reputedly inspired by the Temple of Apollo in Rome, it's a miniature delight: 26m/85ft long, 15m/50ft wide and 17m/55ft high. So pleasing to the eye in its proportions and harmony of line, the building shows Greek influence — not least in the ornamentation, including Corinthian columns. Notice that there are no straight lines: the Romans copied the Greeks, who purposely used slightly convex lines. It was probably not necessary in a building of this size, but the Greeks knew that a slight curvature would correct the optical illusion that straight lines give of curving *inwards*. Like the amphitheatre, the temple has had a chequered past (it *was* used as a house for many years, but also as a stable); it was eventually purchased by the Department of Gard, and restoration began in the early 19th century. Today it houses the **Museum of Antiquities** and exhibits objects contemporary with the temple.

Leaving the Maison Carrée, walk to the north side of the building, to see the small excavation; it shows the floor level 2000 years ago. Then head north on **Rue Auguste**, to the **tourist office** [1] on your right, and pick up any leaflets, maps and brochures you may need.

From the tourist office turn right and continue the short way to **Square Antonin**, where you want to turn left towards the canal you can see on the far side of the traffic lanes (use the zebra crossings on the north side of the square, don't just dash across between the cars). Once safely across, continue along the beautiful, plane-shaded **Quai de la Fontaine** edging the **Canal de la Fontaine**. This is a gorgeous part of the city, linking the centre with the **Jardins de la Fontaine** — surely one of the most beautiful parks in Europe. Created in the 18th century, these

Quai de la Fontaine — one of the most beautiful parts of the city

formal gardens revolve around a **spring** rising on Mont Cavalier to the north and flowing through channelled waterways to the canal you've just strolled along. They are beautifully planted all year round, with nooks and crannies everywhere offering respite from the crowds below (as the lovers will testify). Wide balustraded stairs will take you higher and higher, affording splendid views back to the Maison Carrée and Les Arènes.

Below the balustraded steps, to the far left, is the large restaurant/brasserie/café, Le Pavillion de la Fontaine, with a very large outdoor terrace. This is a delightful place to stop for an early lunch (see page 50). Just to the right of it is the **Temple of Diana**. Dating from the first half of the 2nd century, it was

not originally a temple, but more probably a monument to the nymphs of the nearby spring (*nymphaeum*). But it was converted into a church in the Middle Ages, then later destroyed by fire. Today, only of a nave with a barrel vault and two side corridors remain. The setting is magical — a truly 'romantic ruin'.

Continue up the balustraded steps (or short-cut paths) to reach the octagonal Roman watchtower you saw from the railway station. Despite its elevated position on **Mont Cavalier**, you cannot see it at all on the approach, since it's surrounded by tall trees. But eventually, when the balustrades end, the paths up to it are signposted: '**Tour Magne — vue panoramiqe**'. It may be a bit of a disappointment to find that there is *no view* over the city from the base of the tower — you have to climb the somewhat claustrophobic spiral metal staircase inside (about 150 steps) to the very top — for the advertised panoramic view of the Alpilles and even Mont Ventoux. Originally this 34m/115ft-high tower was part of a pre-Roman line of defences, but was rebuilt and made higher during the reign of Augustus. Even if you haven't the energy to go to the very top, it's still been worth it to rise up to this point — a beautiful area with stately pines.

From the tower go through the green gate and take **Rue Stéphane-Mallarmé** directly opposite. Then turn right on **Rue Rouget de l'Isle** and left on **Rue d'Albenas**. Follow this to a T-junction where the **Castellum** is ahead of you — the circular water tower where the Romans stored water for distribution to the people of Nîmes. Water collected from the Eure spring near Uzès flowed almost 50km/30mi via the Pont du Gard aqueduct (see Walk 7) to this point.

Rising above the Castellum is **Fort Vauban**, a huge edifice built in just one year (1688) to the plans of the famous engineer, from where the Catholic minority could 'control' the larger Huguenot population (after Louis XIV's revocation of the Edict of Nantes). It was later used as a prison, but now belongs to the university.

Head right, downhill, on **Rue de la Lampèze**, go left at the T-junction and then, almost immediately, right on **Rue du Fort**. When you reach lively **Boulevard Gambetta**, follow it to the left for about 500m to the Gothic revival church of **St-Baudille**. Opposite is **Porte d'Auguste**. Also called the '**Porte d'Arles**', this ruin, with a statue of Emperor Augustus, is the triumphal gateway where the **Via Domitia** linking Rome and Cadiz entered Nîmes from the east. The wider central passages were for chariots, the smaller side one for pedestrians.

Keeping Porte d'Auguste to your right, walk west along **Rue Nationale**, past a sign confirming that you are on the old Via Domitia. After 250m, turn left on **Rue des Lombards**. Cross busy **Rue Général Perrier**, a fairly frenetic shopping street (where **Les Halles**, the market described on page 18, is 50m/yds to the right), and continue into **Place aux Herbes**. The square is bristling with shops, cafés and tea shops, full of life — a frenzy on a Saturday afternoon! You are now in **Vieux Nîmes**, with the cathedral of **Notre-Dame-et-Saint-Castor [5]** just to your left. First built in 1096, it was frequently damaged during the religious wars in this area, and completely rebuilt in the 19th century, but the west front still has an attractive Romanesque frieze.

Next to the cathedral is the **Musée du Vieux Nîmes**, located in the 17th-century episcopal palace. There are exhibits about life in the city from the end of the Middle Ages to the present, all organised around a theme — for instance, the history of the textile industry which for centuries (until the 1950s) was the city's chief source of income.

From here you are only some 300m due north of the arena, *but prepare to get lost* — this preserved quarter of the city is a maze of narrow alleyways. From the Place aux Herbes walk south along **Rue des Marchands**, and follow this as it kinks first to the left, then right. Now take the first left turn (**Rue de la Trésorerie**; you should see a sign on one of the buildings).

Heading back across the Esplanade Charles de Gaulle, take one last look back at the Fontaine Pradier, Les Arènes and the Palais de Justice.

Notice, as you cross **Rue des Greffes**, the second turning left, the **Hôtel de Ville** [**6**; Town Hall] behind you to the left, flags a-flutter. (If you want to visit the **Museums of Archaeology and Natural History** [**7**], turn left on Rue des Greffes, past the Town Hall; see plan).

With great relief, you will quickly see the arena ahead. To visit the **Museum of Fine Arts** [**8**], circle the amphitheatre anti-clockwise, cross Rue de la République and continue ahead along Rue Cité-Foulc for about 150m/yds. Otherwise, retrace your steps across the elegant esplanade to the **railway** or **bus station**.

Le Pavillon de la Fontaine

As with our choice for Avignon, it's all about *location* — *not* service or food. This café/brasserie is an oasis of calm in the heart of the city, just beside the Clemenceau canal and facing the Temple of Diana. Watch the fish and the ducks and let the world go by as you

LE PAVILLON DE LA FONTAINE
Quai Georges Clemenceau
(04 66 64 09 93
le-pavillon-de-la-fontaine.pages
perso.orange.fr
daily from 09.00-20.00 €-€€

three menus: a luncheon 'formule' (Mon-Fri) at only 9.50 € — either entrée + dish of the day or dish of the day + dessert; standard menus of all three courses at 16 € and 23 €

wide choice of dishes — from lighter omelettes, carpaccios and kebabs to grilled fish and meats; also snacks and tagliatellis

salads are a speciality — duck breasts with mangoes, seafood, goats cheese, aubergine caviar

'gourmand coffee' — served with a 'tasting' platter of mini fruits, pastries and pudding delicacies

take a (lengthy) break in the large outdoor seating area (service is likely to be *very slow*), enjoying the shady terrace on a hot summer's day or basking in the winter sun.

There's a very large wide range of dishes, from paninis and a beer or crêpes and tea to an exotic three-course, romantic champagne dinner. If it's still on the menu, don't miss the 'café gourmand', with a selection of eight or nine mini-sweets, some with hot chocolate sauce.

restaurants

eat

Seafood salad with a citrus vinaigrette
(salade de fruits de mer en vinaigrette d'agrumes)

At Le Pavillon the seafood salad usually contains giant prawns, smaller shrimp and smoked salmon. But we don't fancy salmon with our citrus vinaigrette so use only shellfish — 500 g tiger prawns, 250 g white crab meat and 250 g lobster. Cold leftover scallops are good too — or crayfish.

First make the vinaigrette by mixing all the ingredients except the garlic and onions in a jar with a lid; shake well to mix, and set aside. *Just before serving,* add the garlic and onions and shake again to mix, then pour into your server.

The very freshest salad greens (we like butterhead lettuce and chicory), some crusty bread and a dry white or rosé wine makes a feast of this meal.

Ingredients (for 4 people)

1 kg mixed cooked seafood
200 g cherry tomatoes
2 basil leaves, torn up
salad greens to taste

for the vinaigrette:

1 tbsp lemon juice
1 tbsp grapefruit juice
2 tbsp orange juice

100 g purée of ripe mangoes
4 tbsp olive oil
salt and pepper
5 g chopped peeled garlic
15 g finely sliced spring onions

recipes

eat

Arles is probably our favourite of the three cities — ever since our first visit when, wandering the alleyways late in the evening, we heard the haunting strains of Bizet's *l'Arlésienne* beautifully played by a lone flautist. The Roman ruins, the fast-flowing Rhône, and the Van Gogh connection all combine for an irresistible atmosphere.

around arles

WALK

3

Start out at the **railway/bus station** in **Arles** [2]. Next door is a **tourist office** [1], but it is only open in summer. Out of the station, turn left on **Avenue Paulin Talbot**. Cross the grassed **Place Lamartine** at the right of its high animated fountain, and go ahead through the ancient ramparts via the **Porte de la Cavalerie** [3]. Walk south on **Rue de la Cavalerie**, going left at the Y-fork. On your right here is the **Fontaine Pichot** [4], shown on page 56.

Now on **Rue Voltaire**, go through **Place Voltaire**. At the next Y-fork, just outside Place Voltaire, go left on **Rue Augustin Tardieu**. Just before the arena, you may want to stop at the **Fondation Van Gogh** [5] on the left, with modern works ranging from paintings and photographs to poems, all inspired by Van Gogh. And perhaps turn left to **Notre-**

Distance: 5km/3mi; all day

Grade: easy, with some steps to climb in the arena and theatre

Equipment: see page 9

Transport: 🚃 to the Gare d'Arles or 🚌 to the *gare routière* (main bus station) — adjacent to the railway station. Or 🚗: park at the railway station (free outdoor parking)

Refreshments: throughout

Market days:
Sat: food market on Blvd des Lices; see page 19
First Wed every month: flea market on Blvd des Lices

Opening times/full entry fee*
All attractions open daily ex 1/1, 1/5, 1/11, 25/12). Arena: 09.00-19.00, 5.50 €; Thermes de Constantin: 09.00-19.00, 3.50 €; St-Trophime Cloisters: 09.00-19.00, 3.50 €; Alyscamps: 09.00-19.00, 3.50 €; Roman Theatre: 09.00-19.00, 3.50 €; Réattu Museum *(cl lunchtime):* 10.00-19.00, 4.00 €; Museon Arlaten *(cl Mon and lunchtime):* 09.30-18.30, 1.00 €; Musée de l'Arles Antique: 9.00-19.00, 5.50 €; Espace Van Gogh 07.30-19.30, free entry; Fondation Van Gogh: 11.00-17.00, 7 €

*High season opening times; in winter open later, often close for lunch — and sometimes stay shut all afternoon!

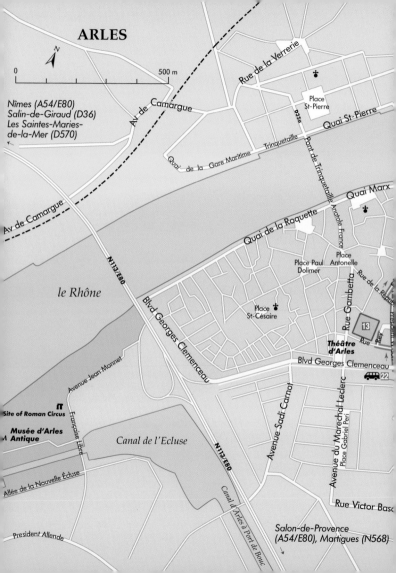

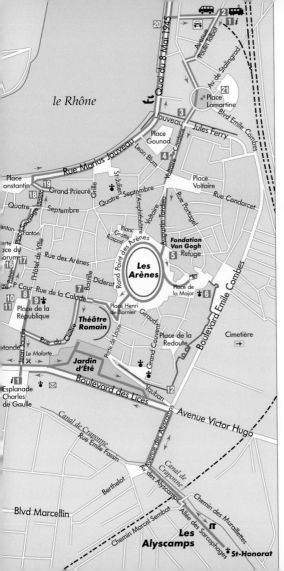

le Rhône

This privately-commissioned fountain, dedicated to Amédée Pichot by his son, incorporates an enamel painting on earthenware representing 'Poetry', in the style of Raphael.

Dame de la Major [6], by the side of which there is a good viewpoint.

Les Arènes, the amphitheatre, dates from the same period as the one in Nîmes (late 1st century) and is very similar in shape and size, being an oval measuring 136 x 107m (446 x 351ft), two storeys high, with 60 arches and seating about 20,000. It was originally taller than the one in Nîmes, but its third story was removed in the 12th century, when the whole arena was transformed into a fortified city of some 200 dwellings. Not only was the third story dismantled to accommodate four watchtowers (only three remain), but building materials taken from the arena were used elsewhere. This accounts for the fact that, despite excavation and restoration beginning in the early 17th century, this arena is slightly less well preserved than the one at Nîmes.

From the platform of the tower above the entrance there is a fine view over the whole structure, the surrounding city and the river — as well as to the ever-present Alpilles chain in the distance. The layout is much the same as that described on page

Climbing inside the arena allows you to see the entire layout — and affords fine views of the countryside.

40, with the 'backstage'. In both of these arenas not only did the dignitaries sit under shady awnings, but the air was perfumed by scented sprays to mask the stench of the animals … and death. There were often orchestras to entertain the guests during 'intervals', food and drink was sold, and the patrons could stroll in the galleries.

As you round the arena clockwise, you first see the tower of St-Trophime, then the cupola above the town hall, then the spire of St-Trophime and, finally, the extensive area of the **Théatre Romain** (**Roman Theatre**) on your left. Dating from the end of the 1st century BC, it has not survived as well as the arena, having been first used as a quarry and eventually disappearing altogether. Rediscovered in the 17th century and excavated, this large theatre (102m/335ft in diameter) would have seated 12,000 spectators. Only two columns and 20 tiers of

seats remain, but a 30,000,000 € project is currently in progress to restore 60 arcades. Excavations here in the 17th century unearthed the famous 'Venus of Arles' given to Louis XIV and a massive sculpture of Augustus; both are now housed in the Musée de l'Arles Antique (see page 62). Squinting up at the top of one of the marble columns, bright against the porcelain-blue sky, one can imagine the theatre's grandiose past.

Continue along **Rue de la Calade** on the north side of the theatre, passing the **Sous-Préfecture** [7] on your right. Then turn left on **Rue du Cloître** (shown above) and descend to **Place de la République**. As you come into the square, most immediately obvious is the eye-catching 17th century **Hôtel de Ville** [8; Town Hall] ahead, with its **cupola/clock tower** — the remains of the original 16th-century building (which was inspired by the mausoleum at Glanum, visited on Walk 5). Eye-catching, too, is the centre-stage **obelisk** with bronze lions heads; this came from the Roman race track (*circus*) west of the

centre, near where the new Musée de l'Arles Antique (see page 62) stands today.

From the Roman Theatre the walk follows two streets on the pilgrims' route to Santiago de Compostela — Rue de la Calade and then Rue du Cloître (opposite), one of the city's enchanting alleyways. Coming into the Place de la République, the cupola on the town hall and the obelisk first catch the eye; St-Trophime, to the right, is less obvious. Inside you will find soaring pillars and Aubusson tapestries.

St-Trophime [9], the real jewel of the square, is much less obvious at first — it's to the right, opposite the town hall. This cathedral is a masterpiece of late Provençal ecclesiastical

Entrance to the Alyscamps

architecture. While the original Romanesque cathedral, dedicated to St Stephen, was built in the 6th century, what is seen today dates mostly from the 12th century, when it was rebuilt and a nave added to house the relics of St Trophimus, to whom it was then consecrated. Most noteworthy is the beautifully decorated **west front**, with about 60 scenes. Inside, the church is most impressive, with its soaring white pillars and Aubusson tapestries detailing the Life of the Virgin.

The **cloisters**, accessed via the Bishops' Palace (to the right of the cathedral), are a delight of Romanesque and Gothic, with scenes from the life of St Trophimus and others from Provençal legends — like that of St Martha subduing the fearsome monster (*tarasque*; see page 6) and the subsequent conversion of Provence to Christianity. The best overview of the cloisters (and the cathedral's belltower) is from the upstairs terrace.

No bars or cafés mar this pristine square, which is bordered on the west side by the **Mairie [10]** and **Chapelle Ste-Anne [11]**. And by now you may be getting a bit peckish — so leave the square by walking due south on **Rue Jean Jaurès**. Soon you should see the **tourist office [1]** ahead, next to a carrousel. But first, take a break on **Boulevard des Lices**, a broad tree-lined avenue which forms the south border of the old city. If it's lunch time, see page 66; otherwise at least stop for a morning drink. Then cross over to the tourist office and collect their good map and whichever brochures take your fancy.

Cross back over Boulevard des Lices and head right through the **Jardin d'Eté**, on the south side of the theatre. Then turn right on **Avenue des Alyscamps** and follow it across the **Canal de Craponne**. Where the avenue bends left, take the walkway at the right of the canal, to the gates of the **Alyscamps**. From Roman times to the late Middle Ages, this was one of the most famous necropoli of the western world, a long avenue, part of the Via Aurelia. One of the tombs, that of St Genesius (a Roman civil servant beheaded in 250 for refusing to persecute the Christians), became the focal point for miracles. More and more people asked to be buried here, so that as early as the 4th century there were several thousand sarcophagi, and by the 13th century three tiers of tombs and 19 chapels. Coffins were sent down the Rhône by boat, with coins for the gravediggers.

Then an abrupt change took place: during the Renaissance the grandest tombs were stolen or given to honoured guests by the city councillors; even monks carted them off to their monasteries. Fortunately, some important sarcophagi were saved and are now exhibited at the Musée de l'Arles Antique (see footnote).

The tombs you see today are all empty and of no artistic value, but they have been assembled into an undeniably impressive avenue (**Allée des Sarcophages**) lined with poplars. Some of these tombs are Greek in style, with a double-pitched roof and four raised corners; the Roman ones have flat tops. At the end of the *allée* is the church of **St Honorat**; its lovely 13th-century two-storey belltower pierced by eight arches.

Retrace your steps to **Boulevard des Lices**. As you come back this way, you'll notice the fortified **Tour des Mourgues [12]** straight ahead, part of the old defensive ramparts. Turn left along the boulevard, passing Le Malarte (see page 66) and after about 250m turn right* on **Rue du Président Wilson**. Take the first left (in front of the hotel Le Relais de Poste), then the first right (**Place Felix Rey**). Now the **Espace Van Gogh [13]** is on

*But to visit the **Musée de l'Arles Antique**, continue a short way further along Clemenceau to the central bus 'station'. Take city bus 1 for 'Barriol' (much more pleasant than walking). This museum — outside the scope of our walk and probably best saved for another day — is housed in a striking triangular building beside the Rhône, near the old Roman racetrack. Built in the 1990s, it brought together collections from two older museums (Pagan Art and Christian Art). Among the displays are the statues of Augustus and the Venus of Arles from the Roman Theatre, and a very large collection of sarcophagi from the Alyscamps.

your left, almost buried by post-card and souvenir shops. *(Before turning in here, note that the large building straight ahead is the Museon Arlatan, the next museum en route.)* A highlight of any visit to Arles, this was originally a hospital where Van Gogh was treated in 1869 after cutting off part of his ear following an argument with Gauguin who had come to visit him. He immortalised it in his painting *Jardin de l'Hôpital à Arles;* today the buildings have been repainted and the gardens re-planted based on his canvas. The

The Espace Van Gogh has been recreated based on the artist's painting.

buildings house a *médiathèque*, as is *de rigueur* these days for exhibition centres, and some arty shops behind the arcades.

Turn left out of the courtyard and continue ahead to the **Museon Arlatan [14]**, facing you on **Rue de la République**. This ethnographic museum was created by Frédéric Mistral with the money awarded when he won the Nobel Prize for Literature in 1904. His aim was to stem the loss of the Provençal language, literature and cultural identity. If you haven't already

Place du Forum, with the scant remains of a temple in the hotel wall, and the Café La Nuit

seen Arlésiennes in traditional dress, you will here. Some 30 rooms hold thematic exhibits — costumes, furnishings, documents, photographs, Mistral's own possessions, and *santons*. It is the most important museum of its kind in Provence.

Turn right out of the museum and right again on **Rue Frédéric Mistral**; then take the first right (**Rue Balze**). From the 17th-century Jesuit church on the right you may be able to gain access to the **Cryptoporticus** [15], but at press date it was closed indefinitely. This underground gallery was designed to support the buildings of the Roman forum directly above, while serving as a storage area as well. Shafts let in air and light, so the gallery could be used more recently as a shelter during WWII air raids.

Keep along Rue Balze and go left on **Rue du Palais** to **Plan de la Cour** and then into **Place du Forum**. On your left, the **Hôtel Nord-Pinus** [16] incorporates two Corinthian columns and a pediment — all that remains of a 2nd-century temple which once rose just to the north of the Roman forum. To your right is the famous **Café La Nuit** [17], another city scene immortalised by Van Gogh. A large bronze statue of Frédéric Mistral looks out over the square.

From the north side of the square, carry on along **Rue de la Place** and then **Rue Sauvage**. When this street bends right, go left on **Rue Dominique Maisto**. On your left are the massive **Thermes de Constantin [18]**. To get into them, you have to circle the building anti-clockwise on a *very* busy street with *no* pavement. *(Just as you turn left here, facing the Rhône, the Musée Réattu, the next museum en route, is just to your right.)* Dating from the 4th century, the baths were part of Emperor Constantine's now-lost riverside palace. How grand that must have been, and what fine views the bathers must have had out over the Rhône!

Opposite the baths, the **Musée Réattu [19]** on **Rue du Grand Prieuré** is located in the 15th-century former priory of the Knights of St John; it is named for the painter Réattu who lived here in the 18th century. This is the city's main art museum, with works from the 16th century to the present. The modern collections include watercolours, engravings and oils by Gauguin, Dufy, Léger, Vlaminck, Vasarely, and Rousseau (to name just a few). There are also large collections of drawings by Picasso done in a variety of techniques and photographs by the likes of Karsh, Izis, Lartigue, Man Ray and Klein.

From the Réattu, turn right and take steps up to the **Rhône embankment**, where Van Gogh painted *Starry Night over the Rhône* (it's said that he wandered here at night with candles on his hat). No less beautiful, it is far less famous than his canvas called simply *Starry Night,* done at St-Rémy. Walk past the **dock for passenger boats** and the sculpted lions [20] which stood on the piers either end of the **Pont aux Lions**, a railway bridge destroyed by bombing in 1944, back to the **railway/bus station**.

Le Malarte

This lively brasserie is just where it should be — right at the heart of the city, on a wide, plane-shaded avenue facing the tourist office

and carrousel. It has had a complete face lift in the last year, since we were last there — much more sophisticated black livery than in this photo.

It's obvious from the selection of dishes shown right that this is a fairly up-market restaurant, and we found the food

LE MALARTE
2, Boulevard des Lices
(04 90 54 56 74
www.grand-cafe-malarte-
restaurant-arles.com
Mon-Wed 12.00-14.30, Thu-Sun
12.00-22.30 €€-€€€

menus at 20 € or 26 €

entrées (each a meal in itself!) feature dishes like risotto with Camargue crayfish, duck breast and *foie gras*

very imaginative **salads**

wood-fired **pizzas** a speciality — 10 different kinds, including gourmet; also **burgers**

grills — beef, lamb, duck, fish or the tiger prawns shown opposite

assorted **cheeses** (with salad)

yummy **desserts** — like crème brûlée with chestnuts and cinnamon

superb. For inspiration, it's worth looking at the photos on their website of the atmosphere and the various dishes currently on offer (there are about 100 photographs). On our last visit, John had the dish of the day, a whole veal kidney (beautifully moist); Pat, who was all 'Provençal'd out', had the grilled tiger prawns in a mild curry sauce (shown opposite).

restaurants

eat

Lobster or crayfish risotto

Seafood risottos feature frequently on the menus of the area's up-market restaurants. *Constant stirring* is the key to this dish!

In a heavy-bottomed skillet, sweat the shallot in the butter and oil. Add the rice and stir with a wooden spoon until thoroughly coated. Then pour in the wine and let it bubble over medium heat until reduced by about two-thirds. Now keep adding the hot stock, a ladleful at a time — so that the rice is always covered but not 'swimming'.

After about 20 min the rice should be swollen and tender: stir in the seafood and heat through. Finally, add the parmesan, salt, pepper, and a dollop of butter. Stir, cover, and let rest for 2 min before serving sprinkled with fresh herbs.

Above, right: lobster risotto at Bistrot Découverte in St-Rémy (see page 86); below: the curried tiger prawns at Le Malarte

Ingredients (for 4 people)

350 g risotto rice, unwashed
1 shallot, minced
180 ml dry white wine
200 g cooked lobster or
    crayfish, diced
1.2 l fish stock, heated
1 tbsp butter
1 tbsp olive oil
2-3 tbsp grated parmesan
salt and pepper to taste

recipes

eat

Les Baux-de-Provence rises on a spur, surrounded by sheer escarpments; the site is extraordinary. In the 13th century it was a famous court of love, in the 14th century the stronghold of evil Raymond de Turenne — whose victims were hurled from the castle into the abyss below. Today it is overrun by tourists; try to visit out of season!

from st-rémy to les baux

WALK

Because of fire hazard, this walk is only possible from 15 September until 14 June (see panel on page 72); the same is true for Walk 5. But both walks are at their best *outside* the blisteringly hot high summer — when you might be tempted to combine them into a long circuit. Unfortunately, if you plan to use public transport, the 'window of opportunity' is very small: there are few buses back from Les Baux outside July and August except for weekends. Taxis are a solution (it's best to arrange this in advance, perhaps at the tourist office in St-Rémy or Les Baux).

Start out in **St-Rémy** at the bustling **Place de la République** (**O**). *(Hint:* You may want to pick up a taxi here to take you up to the lake, saving the first 3km/2mi of the walk.)* On foot, follow the one-way traffic system signposted

Distance: 9km/6mi; 3h
Grade: moderate, with overall ascents of about 300m/1000ft. *IGN map 3042 OT*
Equipment: see page 9; sun protection!
Transport: 🚌 line 57 (Avignon—Arles bus) from the bus station *(gare routière)* in **Avignon** to St-Rémy: 07.40, 08.40, 10.15, 12.15 daily*; journey time about 50min. Or 🚌 line 54 (Arles—Cavillon bus) from the railway station *(gare)* in **Arles** to St-Rémy: 08.13, 11.38**; journey time 45min. Or 🚗 to St-Rémy (park by the tourist office). **Return** on 🚌 line 57 from Les Baux: to St-Rémy or Avignon at 14.53, 17.03, 19.23***; return to Arles at 15.04, 17.09, 19.09. **Outside summer:** 🚗 taxi from Les Baux to St-Rémy, then year-round 🚌 line 57: departs for Avignon daily* at 15.05, 17.15, 19.35, also Mon-Fri at 16.15, 18.15; departs for Arles daily at 14.52, 16.57, 18.57; or 🚌 line 54 at 15.42; journey time 1h.
*not on 14/7, 15/8, 25/12, 1/1; **not Sun; ***daily in Jul and Aug, on weekends from May to end Sep, not from 1/10-10/5
Refreshments: St-Rémy, Les Baux
Market day: Wed in St-Rémy
Opening times/entry fee: Château des Baux, daily 10.00-17.00 (summer 09.00-19.00); 10.50 €

to Les Baux (Avenue Durand-Maillane). Off the first street to the left, on the near side of a large car park, there's a WC, police station and the **tourist office**. As well as stocking interesting leaflets and maps, they may be able to call you a taxi to start the walk if there was none available in Place de la République — or at least arrange for one to collect you at the end. At the end of the one-way system, you pass to the right of the little **Chapelle Notre-Dame de Pitié**; it now displays work given to France by the artist Mario Prassinos. Just under 500m/yds further on, turn right on a narrow road signposted '**Lac des Peirou, Le Barrage**'. Follow this gently uphill, then down (perhaps using marked short-cuts) to the lovely **Barrage des Peiroou** (**1h**), much favoured by picnickers and anglers. Notice, as you approach the lake, a gravel track heading off from the far side of the parking area, past spaces for disabled motorists. Walk 5 uses that route (in case you decide to combine the two walks).

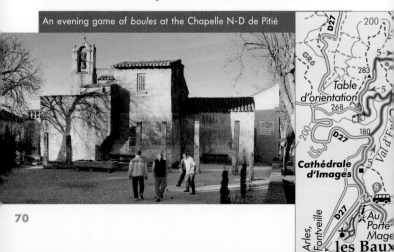

An evening game of *boules* at the Chapelle N-D de Pitié

St-Rémy-de-Provence

See town plan opposite to start

94

100 90

les Antiques

5

100

Glanum

Barrage des Peirou

Vallon de St-Clerg

135

235

5

130

Mas de Gros

306

Mont Gaussier

200

212

D5

300

St-Rémy-de-Provence (inset)

de la blique

Boulevard Victor Hugo

Hoche

8 Mai 1945

Communal

Bistrot Découverte

Avenue Durand Maillane

Avenue Pasteur

St-Rémy-de-Provence

i

5

Avenue Pierre Poujol

Notre-Dame de Pitié (Donation Prassinos)

GR6

D5

0

N

250 m

Avenue Vincent van Gogh

Avenue J d'Arbaud

Av F de Baroncelli

A de la Salle

290

4

200

Tour de Guet

309 5

GR6

4

GR6

5

4

5 289

281

239

5

GR6

0

N

4

200

4

5 4

6

Mas des Lombards

0.5 mi

1 km

200

D27a

4

7

200

D5

e-Provence

Walk *up the road* from the lake for a couple of minutes, until the GR6 turns left on a level forestry track marked AL113. Keep on the road for another 100m/yds, then turn left uphill on a stony track marked AL112 (**❶**). After 12 minutes, a PR path waymarked in yellow goes off to the left: ignore it; follow the track round to the right, to a tarred area with a **cistern** (**❷**; **1h15min**). Continue straight ahead along the tar, ignoring a track descending to the right. Looking left now, you'll see the huge ORTF relay equipment on the bluff of La Caume.

Ignore a path to the right and then two tracks going off to the left; keep on the main track, which bends sharply to the right. You enjoy good views to the north, before the track turns southwards again. At this point (**1h30min**) the main track continues ahead, but we fork right uphill on a footpath — which may have both GR and PR waymarks. (This path gives super views of the north from a crest. If you prefer to avoid the climb, or if a *mistral* is blowing, stay on the track and fork right when you come to a T-junction after 250m.)

So far the ascent has been imperceptible, but now we *do*

Fire hazard

Because the summers are getting much hotter (and arriving much earlier), the Alpilles — in common with many other forested areas in France — are now off-bounds to walkers from 15 June until 15 September. A **Parc naturel régional des Alpilles** has been created to protect (and promote) the range: see **www. parc-alpilles.fr**, only in French unfortunately). During high summer, the park organises guided walks outside the protected zone — to olive groves, vineyards and the like (details from the tourist office at Les Baux or St-Rémy).

The trail proper — into the Alpilles — begins here at Lake Peiroou. If you visit in summer when the main walk is off-bounds, you could walk to this lovely lake and then on to Les Antiques and Glanum — finishing up with the 'Van Gogh walk' described on page 84. Below: landscape near the 2h15min-point; view up to Les Baux village

climb. In about six minutes we reach the top with its fine views and gale-force winds. Five minutes later we're back down on the main track. Continue southwest along the main track now, past a minor cart track off to the right. Two minutes along,

ignore a numbered fire track coming in from the left and then a track off right to the fire watchtower (❸; **Tour de Guet**); keep straight ahead.

Now we are going to part company with

The lovely church of St-Vincent at Les Baux. If you visit during the Christmas holidays, you'll see this decorated cart: at Christmas midnight mass, shepherds use it to lead a newborn lamb to the altar.

the GR and take a much more attractive path. This path is *not way-marked*, so follow the notes carefully. Five minutes/300m past the track up to the watchtower, the main track

74

describes a deep U-bend, and you come to a junction of paths and tracks (**1h55min**): a path comes down from the watchtower on the right, and another path goes out left to a triangulation point. Leave the main track here (it is the route of Walk 5): take the track to the left of the main track, but to the right of the path to the triangulation point. You are walking parallel with the main track, but descending. After 70m/yds downhill, turn left on another track — the first one you come to. Now you're heading in the direction of the triangulation point, and soon the track becomes a lovely grassy footpath. Not far along, a path comes down from the triangulation point and joins you from the left.

After descending for about 15 minutes meet a wide stony crossing path (**❹**; **2h15min**) and turn left; you may see some old waymarks underfoot. In two minutes go round a chain barrier, then meet a surfaced track and turn left (**❺**; above a house). Pass a few houses on the right and immediately come to a junction (**❻**). Turn right, gradually descending. Another PR walk, waymarked in yellow, comes in from the left after 600m/yds, and 100m/yds further on you meet the D27a (**❼**; **2h30min**). Turn right; now you have to follow this road just over 1.5km uphill, but all along there are fine views to the bauxite mines and Les Baux rising on the cliffs.

Continue uphill past the **bus stop** (**❽**) and some parking areas, then fork left. You pass a grocer's and the **taxi office** on the left. The **tourist office** is just inside the main entrance to **Les Baux** (**3h**). Hopefully you've set out early enough to explore the village and citadel — and enjoy a great meal!

Au Porte Mages

A real find — not only is this one of only a couple of year-round restaurants at Les Baux, but we found it exceptionally good. John claimed his duck Rossini (with *foie gras*) was one of the best meals ever; Pat ate *all* of her *galette,* and then we splurged on a huge (shared) pear sorbet drenched in pear liqueur. We'll be back!

Still charmingly decorated for the Christmas holidays, inside all was stone walls, warm red tablecloths, and very friendly service. Outside there is a lovely shady terrace for summer, when the menu is lighter — with more salads and puff pastry dishes.

Succulent duck Rossini — with pan-fried *foie gras*, Provençal tomatoes, ratatouille and chips. All gluten-free, but on (easily removed) toast ... see 'Hint' inside the back cover!

AU PORTE MAGES
Rue Porte Mage (inside the village gate, just past the tourist office, on the left) (04 90 54 40 48
daily all year 11.30-21.30 (cl Mon from Nov till 11 Feb) €€

daily **menu**: three courses 24 €

enormous **à la carte** selection (5 pages), featuring everything from **Provençal specialities** (bull steak, grilled lamb with herbs, tripe sausage, duck) to **puff pastries** filled with fish or meat; 8 different **salads** (with cheese, fish or meat); 15 savoury pancakes (*galettes*, made with buckwheat flour)

for **dessert** 20 sweet pancakes, 15 ice creams, 18 'gourmand' ice cream and liqueur combinations — to say nothing of the standard tarts and rich chocolate confections

restaurants

eat

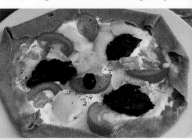

Galette de sarrasin garrigue (buckwheat crêpe with Provençal filling)

Put all the crêpe ingredients into a mixer and whizz for 1 min to make a smooth, thin batter. Cover with a tea towel and leave for 2 h. Then preheat the oven to 200°C/400°F/ gas mark 6.

Use a paper towel to *lightly* grease a crêpe (or omelette) pan, then heat until a couple of drops of water sprinkled into the pan sizzle. Pour in just enough batter to thinly coat the bottom (swirl the pan until it does so). Cook for 2 min, or until the top of the crêpe dries. Flip and cook the other side for 1 min, or until lightly browned. Repeat until all the batter is used, keeping the cooked crêpes warm.

Arrange the cream, cheese and tomatoes as shown in the photograph, then fold in the edges as illustrated. Place on baking trays and heat in the oven until the cheese melts (about 15 min). Then put on table-spoonful of *tapenade,* dot with olives, sprinkle with the herbs and bake for another minute or two — just to warm the *tapenade* before serving (perhaps with a green salad).

Ingredients (for 4-5 *galettes*)
150 g buckwheat flour
1 egg
1 tsp olive oil
1/4 tsp salt
250 ml water
20 g butter or oil for frying
for the filling
1 'log-style' goats' cheese *(buche de chevre),* thinly sliced
1 pot soured cream
4 small tomatoes, cut into thin wedges
jar ready-made *tapenade* (eg Rick Stein's) — or see recipe on page 115
handful of pitted black olives
herbes de Provence (garnish)

recipes

eat

This lovely walk takes you from the magnificently-sited citadel of Les Baux to the Roman sites of Les Antiques and Glanum outside St-Rémy. The walk ends by following in the footsteps of Van Gogh to the village centre. Those with lots of energy can combine this with Walk 4 — a circuit that avoids all the transport problems.

from les baux to st-rémy

WALK

5

Les Baux is one of the busiest tourist venues in Provence; *do try* to beat the crowds to the citadel (open from 10.00; 09.30 in summer) before starting this walk! **The walk starts** at the **bus stop** (**O**) on the D27a: head over the pass and downhill towards 'Fontvieille' and 'Arles'. Joining the D27, go right for 'Maillane', ignoring the left turn for Fontvieille and Arles. Soon you pass the **Cathédrale d'Images** (**❶**) and some bauxite mines. Just beyond the sign denoting the **exit from Les Baux (20min)**, turn right on a track and walk to the right of a chain barrier (prohibiting vehicles). After climbing for less than 15 minutes, come to a T-junction with a stony track and turn left, still climbing (here you join a PR route waymarked in yellow). Three minutes uphill you round a bend and have a most magnificent view over to

Note: This walk is only possible outside high summer due to fire hazard; see paragraph one of the main text on page 69.

Distance: 12km/7.4mi; 3h30min

Grade: quite easy, with ascents of under 150m/500ft. *IGN map 3042 OT*

Equipment: see page 9; sun protection!

Transport: 🚌 57 (Avignon—Arles* **summer** bus timetable); departs **Avignon** bus station 07.40, 10.15, 12.15; journey time 55min; departs **Arles** 07.55, 10.25, 12.20; journey time 55min. **Outside summer**, 🚌 line 57 from **Avignon** or 🚌 line 54 from **Arles** to St-Rémy (see page 69), or 🚗 car. Then **taxi** to Les Baux (pre-arrange at the St-Rémy tourist office). For **return times** from St-Rémy to Avignon (🚌 57) or Arles (🚌 54) see page 69.
*daily in Jul and Aug, only on weekends from May to end Sep, not from 1/10-10/5

Refreshments: St-Rémy, Les Baux

Market day: Wed in St-Rémy

Opening times/entry fees: Château des Baux (see page 69); Glanum, daily ex Mon from 10.00-17.00 (09.30-18.00 between 1/4-30/9); 8 € adults, 5 € children

the left, across the Val d'Enfer and to Les Baux: the old mines are in foreground on other side of valley, with the village and the citadel behind them. The gentle Vallon de la Font spreads out to the right of the citadel.

Some 25 minutes off the D27 meet a tarmac road and cross straight over: climb the steep path opposite, to the vandalised remains of a once-beautiful *table d'orientation* (viewing table; ➋; **45min**). Now just a concrete stump marks this lovely **viewpoint**. Unless it is very hazy, you will have good outlook to the Camargue and the Rhône Valley, the Lubéron and Mont Ventoux. From the viewpoint walk down the wide track. Join the tarmac road and follow it to the left. When the road runs out, keep straight ahead on a tarmac lane, behind a chain barrier. Stalwart yellow mullein blooms here in summer. Five minutes along, at a Y-fork, ignore the concreted **fire point** (➌) up to the right; keep left along the track. Ten minutes later ignore the overgrown track on the right; keep left on the main track, ignoring another faint track off left after a few paces.

Half an hour from the viewpoint (**1h15min**) you round a U-bend below the fire watchtower (➍; **Tour de Guet**). Five minutes later pass a track up left to the watchtower and two minutes after that a **path up left** (➎; Walk 4 descends it); keep right along the track here. Some 150m/yds further on, where a fainter track goes downhill to the right, keep left with the red and white flashes of the GR6 on the level track. It curls around to

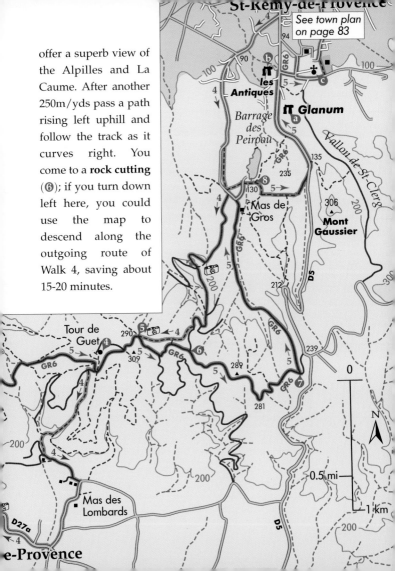

St-Rémy-de-Provence

See town plan on page 83

offer a superb view of the Alpilles and La Caume. After another 250m/yds pass a path rising left uphill and follow the track as it curves right. You come to a **rock cutting** (**6**); if you turn down left here, you could use the map to descend along the outgoing route of Walk 4, saving about 15-20 minutes.

les Antiques

Glanum

Barrage des Peirou

Vallon de St-Clerg

Mas de Gros

Mont Gaussier

Tour de Guet

GR6

Mas des Lombards

e-Provence

Les Antiques, on the D5 south of St-Rémy — the arch (above) and mausoleum (right) survive from Glanum, the site across the road.

But we continue past the cutting, keeping to the GR6. Looking down left through the trees, soon you will spot Lake Peiroou, with the spire of St-Rémy's church behind it. Ignore any grassy downhill tracks either side of the main track. The downhill track you want comes up about 20 minutes past the cutting — only about 150m/yds short of the D5. Head left downhill with the red and white flashes of the GR6 (**❼**; **1h55min**), as the track you have been following continues ahead to the D5.

This pine-shaded, stony track takes you to a U-bend of the tarmac road to the lake. Turn right, following 'Barrage' and, from the parking area for the **Barrage des Peiroou** (**2h15min**), follow the GR6 to the right on a gravel track. But *be sure to keep right* at the Y-fork (**❽**) just 50m along: *do not follow the GR6 to the left* unless you are very adventurous and have a head for heights — it's what the French call a '*parcours sportif*', with some scrambling and a ladder. This wide path (keep left 150m/yds along) rises and falls to the **D5**, where you turn left. St-Rémy is now only about half an hour away. But first you pass the extensive **Glanum** (ⓐ) excavations, covering five acres. The area was probably first settled by Celtic-Ligurians (Glanics) in the 6th century BC, at the site of a sacred spring. Greeks came later, and then the Romans. But the wealthy city was overrun by the Barbarians in the 3rd century and abandoned. Whether or not you visit Glanum, you'll pass **Les Antiques** (ⓑ) just beside the road: a mausoleum and triumphal arch — two of Glanum's well-preserved remains.

Then, rather than keeping to the D5, take road almost opposite Les Antiques, the Chemin des Carrières

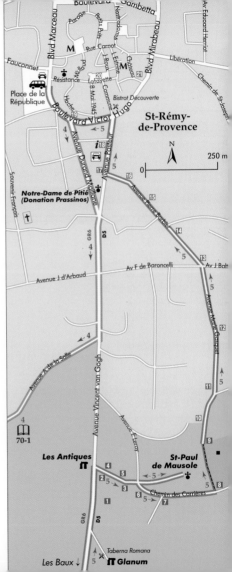

(with a fingerpost to 'Eygalières' and signs for the 11th-century chapel and cloister of St-Paul de Mausole). This leads to a much prettier route back into town, walking in the 'Universe of Van Gogh'. Obviously this is a marketing ploy of the St-Rémy tourist office — an 'art route' as opposed to a wine route. Very few of the reproduction plaques are placed where he actually painted the canvases, since the immediate area is so changed by housing. But the overall effect captures the timeless

A statue of the artist, with sunflowers, greets you outside the chapel of St-Paul de Mausole with its lovely square bell tower.

Typical honey-hued *hôtel* at St-Rémy. The plane-shaded, elegant façades of the town's buildings — some of them dating from the 15th or 16th century, contribute enormously to the atmosphere of the avenues and boulevards.

essence of this part of provence — cypresses, olive groves, and the Alpilles.

There are 21 reproductions, but unless you visit Glanum the first plaque you will encounter is No 2 *(Les Oliviers)*, just inside this road. They lead you first to **St-Paul de Mausole**, where Van Gogh was hospitalised (it serves much the same function today and is considerably larger). Use the plan on page 83 to find all the reproductions and make your way back to the **Place de la République** in **St-Rémy** (**9**; **3h30min** — or much longer, if you visited Glanum).

Promenade dans l'univers de Vincent van Gogh

7 Les blés jaunes avec cyprès
(National Gallery, London, Grande Bretagne)

Beside each reproduction are explanatory notes in French and English, as well as a map of the route with all the numbered plaques.

85

Bistrot Découverte

Of the 60 or so restaurants in St-Rémy, this one is centrally placed on Victor Hugo, a few steps from the tourist office. It was set up by a husband/wife team, Claude and Dana and has been widely admired ever since. Claude worked in England with both Raymond Blanc and Marco Pierre White. With such a pedigree, this is not an inexpensive restaurant, but the luncheon *formule* is good value.

The key here is seasonality: when we last visited, asparagus was in season, so there were some special dishes built around it. Naturally the *carte* changes quite frequently, so the mini-menu here just gives an idea of what might be available.

The good house white is from the nearby Val-dition estate; you can buy some from the wine cellar downstairs *(take care on the steep steps)*.

BISTROT DECOUVERTE
19, Boulevard Victor Hugo (04 90 92 34 49; www.bistrotdecouverte.fr
open daily all year for lunch and dinner
€€-€€€

lunch *formule* (dish of the day + dessert of the day + bio coffee) at 16.90 €; menus (two courses 27 €; three courses 32 €)

4 entrées (like Corsican *charcutérie*, frogs' legs, asparagus risotto, swordfish carpaccio)

3 salads (meals in themselves!)

6 mains, including sweetbreads in port sauce, turbot, suckling pig, lamb with Provençal herbs, veal steak in parmesan cream sauce

cheeses from St-Rémy, and **5 desserts** plus **one dish of the day at £12.90** and **more suggestions from the blackboard** (including line-caught fish of the day)

restaurants

eat

Filets de loup de mer au fenouil (sea bass fillets with fennel)

John had this fish of the day from the blackboard menu (Pat had the lobster risotto shown on page 67). Although his serving had two fillets, we think one per person is enough!

First prepare the fennel for braising. Cut off the feathery leaves, small stems and the tough base. Cut the bulb in half lengthwise and remove the tough core from each side. Rinse under cold water.

In a suitably sized pan, sweat the fennel bulbs carefully in about 100 ml olive oil, then (without discarding the oil) add *barely enough* stock to cover, and braise over medium heat for 30-40 min, until tender. (If the fennel starts to dry out, add a little hot water.) When ready, drain, season, and keep warm.

Assemble the sauce ingredients in a jar, screw on the lid, and shake vigorously until thoroughly mixed.

Dust the fish lightly with flour and fry skin side first, until crispy. Carefully turn to cook through. Then assemble as shown above and drizzle with olive oil/lemon sauce.

Ingredients: (for 4 people)
4 fillets of sea bass
2 whole fresh fennel
250 ml fish or vegetable stock (or water)
olive oil for braising and frying
flour for dusting
salt and pepper to taste
for the sauce
200 ml top-quality olive oil
juice of 1 lemon
1 tbsp parsley, finely chopped
1 tsp salt
1 tsp water

recipes
eat

The plain below La Montagnette, a pocket-sized mountain near the Rhône, is the setting for a delightful walk through woodlands and beside flower-filled olive groves, with the additional interest of a visit to the abbey of St-Michel-de-Frigolet and the charming village of Barbentane with its exquisite château.

barbentane and frigolet

WALK

Start out at the **bus stop** in front of **La Poste** (**O**) in **Barbentane**: continue west, looking to the right immediately along the **Rue des Pénitents**, to see the **Château de Barbentane** (**a**) — unfortunately no longer open to the public. Continue past the **Mairie** and the Hôtel St-Jean; then, just in front of a car park, go left on the *lower* of the two roads with 'no entry' signs. Walking against the one-way traffic, keep on this road past the **fire station**, until you come to another **car park** on your right (**b**; about **10min**). Up to your left, there is an old windmill, the **Moulin de Brétoule** (**c**).

From the right-hand side of the car park, take the yellow-waymarked track behind the barrier (just to the left of a house and with a 'MD200' fire bollard at the left). Ignore all turnings off

Distance: 12.3km/7.6mi; 3h15min if travelling by bus; somewhat less if travelling by car

Grade: easy, with ascents/descents of about 150m/500ft overall. It helps to have a good sense of direction both at the start of the walk and on leaving Frigolet, as there are many woodland tracks. *IGN map 3042 OT*

Equipment: see page 9

Transport: 🚌 56 (Avignon—Tarascon* bus, Mon-Sat only); departs **Avignon** bus station 08.05, 12.10; journey time 30min; departs **Tarascon** *train* station 13.00, 18.55; journey time 22min. Alight at the bus stop called 'La Place' in the centre of Barbentane. **Returns** from the same stop to Avignon at 13.22, 19.14; to Tarascon at 17.04, 18.27. Or 🚗: park at **b** (near the Moulin de Brétoule; see second paragraph of the text).
*with connecting buses to Nîmes

Refreshments en route: at Saint-Joseph, in Barbentane and at St-Michel-de-Frigolet

Opening times/entry fees: Abbey church, St-Michel church and shop at Frigolet generally open all year 08.00-11.00, then 14.00-18.00; entry free (www.frigolet.com). **Note: the Château de Barbentane is not open to the public.**

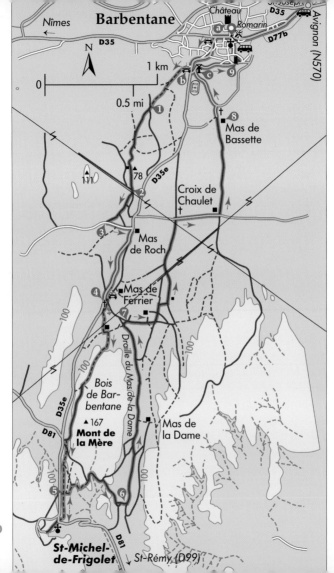

Barbentane

Nîmes ←

Château

Romarin

D35

D77b

Avignon (N570)

1 km

N

0 0.5 mi

① Mas de Bassette ⑧

▲78 D35e

▲111

Croix de Chaulet †

② Mas de Roch ③

④ Mas de Ferrier ⑦

100

100 Draille du Mas de la Dame

D35e

Bois de Bar-bentane

▲167 Mont de la Mère

D81

100 100

Mas de la Dame

001

⑤ ⑥

D81

St-Michel-de-Frigolet

St-Rémy (D99) →

this track until you come to a major, staggered junction (**①**; **25min**), where you keep right uphill. Ignore a waymarked track off right four minutes later; keep ahead, passing a yellow 'X' on a tree on the left. Walk between a **huge boulder** (left; 78m) and a **cottage** (**c**; right).

Some 300m/yds further on, as you pass under **power lines** (**②**; **40min**), keep straight ahead, ignoring a track to the right and another running downhill to the left. Pass two tracks off left in quick succession, then take the *third* left turn (**③**) — *a dirt road which curves in front of you.* This comes down to the D35e at Mas de Roch. Turn right on the road and follow it to **Mas de Ferrier**. Just past here, turn left to a large shaded parking area just at the start of a motorable track, the **Draille du Mas de la Dame** (**④**; **55min**).

From the **parking area** head south on a stony track running not far to the left of the D35e; you pass *between* a **well** on the left and a **shrine** on the right almost imme-

The unmistakable 19th-century spires of Frigolet. The abbey takes its name from the Provençal word for thyme, *ferigoulo*. You'll be constantly crushing this perfumed herb underfoot during this walk. Here's a hint for an *apéritif* you could make, in France or back home. Soak two sprigs of fresh, flowering thyme in a litre of dry white wine for two weeks *(being sure to reseal the bottle tightly)*. Then strain the wine, add a little liquid honey, shake gently but thoroughly, and let 'age' for a month before enjoying.

diately. Just before the track rejoins the D35e, take a wide path on the left. After passing to the right of a large **building foundation in ruins**

(**1h**), turn left at a T-junction. After 30m/yds, go right uphill on another path in the **Bois de Barbentane** — the prettiest woodland path on the walk, almost jungle-like in places. After passing through a clearing and going round a wire barrier, cross the scruffy forestry works area, bearing right on a forestry track.

Once inside the 19th-century crenellations of the outer wall, St-Michel-de-Frigolet has more subdued charms — like cobbled walkways, old façades, and the simple 12th-century church of St-Michel.

From now on, *just keep to the left of the D35e,* whether on track or path. Go through a **tall hedge of cypresses** (**5**) and continue 250m/yds to the abbey of **St-Michel-de-Frigolet** (**1h25min**). The austere 19th-century spires seen on the approach are not very appealing, but you are in for a surprise! Inside the lavishly decorated main church you'll find the original 11th-century abbey, now an apse off the north aisle. This little gem, the chapel of **Notre-Dame-du-Bon-Remède**, has beautiful gilt panelling. Then take some time to wander along the shaded walkways and in the lovely grounds (with a herb garden). There used to be a superb café/restaurant here (La Treille) housed in the old bakery); it closed, and its successor was a big disappointment when we ate there a couple of years ago, but it reopened in summer 2018 under new management and we await reports!

After your visit to the abbey, return to the **cypress hedge** and turn right in front of it. Just past the end of the hedge, turn left on a crossing path. Follow this for 70m/yds, then turn right down a clear but narrow path into a gully. A pretty path through *maquis* takes you out of the gully, then dips again — to the hairpin bend of a track (**1h20min**). Turn right, beginning to round the stony hillock of **Mont de la Mère**.

At a fork 200m/yds further on, go right. After another 250m/yds, turn 90° left at a junction. Reaching a T-junction 100m/yds further on, go left. Now you are back on the **Draille du Mas de la Dame** (**6**) and can continue straight ahead, with no more forks to worry about. You pass a *gîte* on the left and then the **Mas de la Dame** on the right (**1h50min**). The *Draille* runs back to Mas de Ferrier. But you are not going back to the main road, so after 900m/0.6mi, *watch for the back of a road sign on your left* (it may bear a yellow 'X'): turn right here, then right again (**❼**; **2h05min**).

After 250m/yds, beyond an olive grove on the left, you

come to another *mas* and a junction: go left here, ignoring tracks to the right and straight ahead. Pass a second entrance to the same estate (on the left) and ignore a track to the right just opposite it. But at the next, Y-fork, go right. After 100m/yds, at a T-junction, go left. Pass a shed in a pretty grassy area on the right and come to crossroads at a clearing, with **power lines** overhead. Keep straight ahead, downhill. When a track comes in from the left, behind you, keep right downhill.

Moulin de Brétoule

Walk to the left of a cherry orchard and under more **power lines**. Just before an iron cross (**Croix de Chaulet; 2h30min**), turn right on a country lane. Over to the left, across fields, you can see the Tour Angelica at Barbentane on a slight, wooded rise; dating from 1365, it's the keep of the former castle. Some 400m/yds along, turn left on a cart track (opposite a sign 'M0104'). This route is a delight of colourful hedgerows and olive groves.

Just beyond **Mas de Bassette** (❽; **2h50min**) go straight ahead on a tarred road, passing an **iron cross** atop a mound on the right. Rise to a T-junction and turn left on the **Chemin Moulin de Brétoule** through a modern housing estate. Keep on this road past a **football pitch** (behind cypresses on the left) and then an olive grove (also on the left). At another T-junction, with the old **windmill** seen earlier up to the right (**2h55min**), turn left and walk to the main road opposite the **car park** (ⓑ).

You *could* return from here to your car if you parked there, but it's worth following the notes below for bus travellers, to see a bit of Barbentane.

If you came by bus, turn *right* here, following yellow waymarks along a wooded road. You pass the **Tour Angelica** (❾), beyond which steps lead you down to a route through the old village. Walking via the **Place de l'Église**, you emerge through an arch (the **Porte Calendrale**) on the main village street diagonally opposite the **Poste** and the **bus shelter** (◯; **3h15min**. Wait for your return bus on the opposite side of the road from where you got off earlier in the day. If you parked by the old windmill, use the notes on page 89 to return to your car.

Le Romarin

La *patronne*, Martine, has been catering since 1986, and this restaurant is very popular with locals who appreciate the traditional food and fair prices. It's still a tiny place, but in 2018 underwent what she calls a 'relookage'(!), with the results below — a shock: we were used to her old-style décor, with herbs and pressed flowers on the walls and Provençal-fabric tablecloths.

But the food is still delicious (see a photo of their *salade gourmande* on page 139). The only drawback is that there is no outside terrace for summer.

LE ROMARIN
11, Avenue Bertherigues, Barbentane
☎ 04 90 95 58 43; restoromarin.fr
all year, closed Mon, Sun dinner, hours 12.00-14.30 (Sun brunch from 11.00) and 19.30-21.00 €-€€

formule at 13.50 € (entrée + main course or main + dessert), but if you eat à la carte and choose both an entrée and a main course (average price 23 €), dessert is free

traditional French/Provençal fare

entrées — salads, *escargots*, vegetarian buffet, patés, terrines, *charcutérie*

snacks/sandwiches/pastas

specialities: lamb shanks with garlic preserve (see recipe), steaks, osso bucco with saffron rice, tripe sausage in pastry case with grain mustard

cheese plate, **home-made sweets**

picnics to take away (three courses + wine for 18 €)

restaurants

eat

Souris d'agneau confites à l'ail (lamb shanks with garlic)

We have no idea how Martine made this delicious dish, and she was too busy to be asked! Here's our version; *everything* contains garlic, but the long cooking leaves it deliciously sweet.

Preheat the oven to 150°C/300°F/gas mark 2. Tuck 1 sliced garlic clove into each shank. Place the shanks (with the other peeled cloves and the thyme) in a large heavy-bottomed skillet and brown on all sides, *being sure not to let the oil or garlic burn*.

Season the shanks and wrap individually in thick foil, together with half an onion, some more thyme leaves, and the oiled cloves from half a head of unpeeled garlic. Roast in the foil for 2 h.

Unwrap, discard the foil, onions and herbs, and place the shanks and garlic in a roasting pan. Raise the heat to 200°C/400°F/gas mark 6 and roast for another half hour, until the meat and garlic cloves are nicely browned.

Serve as here: with the roasted garlic cloves, green beans braised with garlic, and *pommes dauphinoises* (*gratin* of baked sliced potatoes with cream and yet more garlic).

Ingredients (for 4 people)

4 x 200 g lamb shanks
3 whole heads of garlic, separated into cloves: peel and slice 8 cloves, toss the others (unpeeled) in olive oil and set aside
2 onions, halved
olive oil for initial frying
handful of fresh thyme leaves (pulled off the stalks)
salt and ground pepper

recipes

A UNESCO World Heritage site, the Pont du Gard is a colossal work of art, to be admired from all angles, and in different lights. Plan to devote a full day to this beautiful and varied five-star walk, taking a long break by the Gardon and spending some time at the fascinating visitors' centre and in the pretty village of Vers.

pont du gard

WALK

Start the walk at the **bus stop called 'Cave'** (⚪) on the southern fringes of **Vers**. The **wine co-op** is only about 70m/yds away, but not visible from here; we pass it later. With your back to the bus stop, turn left and follow the road to a T-junction in front of the **cemetery** (❶). Turn right here, cross the **railway**, then turn right again immediately. After 100m/yds, turn left on a cart track (initially surfaced) through vineyards, cherry orchards and olive groves.

Cross the D981 and continue (25m to the left) towards 'La Bégude St-Pierre'. Then turn left on **Chemin du Passeur**, joining the **GR6/63**. As you pass the **Hotel La Bégude St-Pierre** (a lovely place to stay), turn right in front of its car park and continue straight on, past the ruined **Chapelle St-Pierre** (❷; **25min**) in a field of golden cereals and poppies.

Distance: 8.6km/5.3mi; 2h10min

Grade: easy, with ascents/descents of little more than 100m/330ft overall. Some agility needed on the 'Panorama' path. Avoid weekends and holidays, when the Pont du Gard is swarming with people. Yellow PR and some red and white GR waymarking. Limited shade. *IGN map 2941 E*

Equipment: see page 9; swimwear

Transport: 🚌 ine A15 from **Avignon** bus station to the wine co-op in Vers ('Cave' bus stop): departs 08.45 and 11.40 daily; journey time 45min. Return buses at 17.28 and 18.42 Mon-Fri, 18.52 Sat and Sun. 🚌 line B21 from **Nîmes** bus station to Vers: daily at 07.30, 11.30 and 13.30. Returns at 15.49 and 18.14 Mon-Fri *only*. Journey times about 1h. Or 🚗 to Vers.

Refreshments: Vers; cafés on the left bank of the Gardon and cafés and restaurant on the right bank (see pages 105-106)

Opening times/entry fee: The Pont du Gard site is open daily all year from 09.00 until 18.00 in winter, 22.00 in summer (23.00 Jul/Aug); 8.50 € basic rate, up to 15.50 € to take in all amenities — but a multitude of passes and special offers for families, groups, students, etc.

Coming to a T-junction, turn left past a house and through a **metal barrier**, to continue on the lane. When you reach a **barrage of signposts** (❸; **40min**), keep to the lane along the GR63 (signpost: '**Pont du Gard 0,8km**'). ('Pont du Gard' is also signposted half-right here via the GR6; this is the return route.)

When the tarmac ends, descend ahead to a walkway : the **Pont du Gard** (❹; **45min**) is to your right. Follow the paved path and cross the bridge. On the far side, take steps up to the right, to a fine view of the river and bridge. At the top of the

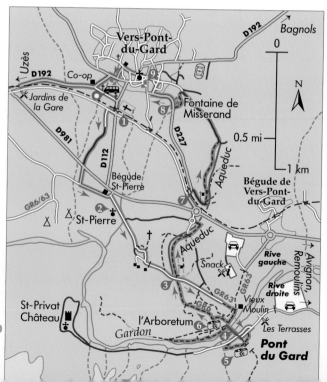

steps, turn right for '**panorama**', following GR waymarks. Beyond the **viewpoint** (**5**; **52min**), continue on this path which zigzags back down to the river.

Meeting the lane on the south side of the bridge, turn right, walk below one of the arches and after 100m/yds, turn back sharp right to cross back to the *rive gauche* (left bank). From here you could explore the arboretum just above the river for as long as you like. But the main walk goes straight ahead up steps (signpost: '**GR6/63, PR41**'). From here on, the maze of paths through the *garrigues* can be confusing, so keep a close eye on the yellow and red and white waymarks; *you should always be on a strong, clear, waymarked path*. But first make a short detour left, to the left bank's **panorama** (**6**; **1h15min**).

The route goes through a beautiful wood of holly and holm oak, where the yellow and red fruits of the strawberry tree and pink cistus shine against the dark foliage. Soon remains of the old aqueduct begin appearing on the left.

When you come back to the **signposts** first encountered at the 40min-point (**3**; **1h25min**), cross straight over the lane (signpost: '**Vers**'). There are even more substantial remains on this stretch. At a crossing with a lane on the left and a track to the right, go straight ahead up a steep dirt path. There is a beautiful setting not far along, with rocks placed in a circle beneath a huge holm oak on the right — a perfect picnic spot.

Approaching the D981, walk 100m/yds to the left on the track, to a small roundabout. Take the steps down the steep embankment, cross the D981 *carefully,* and then go straight ahead on a road signposted '**Carrières de Vers-Est**'. Cross the

Some of the finest views of the aqueduct can be had from the riverside on the *rive gauche*, near the nature trail

railway (**7**; **1h45min**) and immediately turn right up a motorable gravel track. At the top of the rise, make a U-turn to the left (signpost: '**Fontaine Menestière**'), then keep left at a Y-fork. The arches and buttresses of the ruined aqueduct are still beside you. Keep left at two more Y-forks and then turn left at a T-junction; *watch the yellow waymarks on this stretch!*

Finally the aqueduct remains end and you come onto a

motorable track: keep straight ahead. Just as this track becomes tarred (by a **fire hydrant** on the left), turn left on a pretty woodland path. It comes down to the D227 at the **Fontaine de Misserand** (**8**). Turn right on the road, then take the first right

The substantial remains of the old aqueduct passed near the end of the walk.

uphill (**Rue du Lavoir**). Keep straight ahead past any turn-offs. At a T-junction go left downhill (**Chemin des Crozes**). Continue to the **Place de la Fontaine** in **Vers** (**9**; **2h15min**), a lovely cool spot with a *lavoir* surrounded by plane trees.

Before moving on to catch your return bus, take some time to look around Vers or have some refreshments in one of the bars/cafés. The village website (www.vers-pont-du-gard.fr) has some good ideas on local walks for those spending time in the area: under 'Vie pratique' click on 'Traductions', then on 'en anglais': this brings up a pdf called 'Tourism'. After an introduction to some village history, there are descriptions of 11 walking routes around Vers.

When you are ready to move on, face the *lavoir* and head right towards 'Centre Village', following the one-way traffic arrows. You pass to the right of the **church**. At the top of this road, go half-right into **Rue des Ecoles** (with the 'no entry' sign). At the **school** (on your right), turn left on **Rue de Palezieux**, signposted to Uzès. After the road bends right, take the second left turn ('Uzès'); on your left is the **Lavoir de Font d'Izière**. Coming to a T-junction, with the **wine co-operative** on your right, turn *left* towards 'Remoulins'. (The restaurant La

Petite Gare is about 500m/yds to the *right* along this road.) You pass an **iron crucifix** on the left and then come to the **'Cave' bus stop** for your return journey (**O**; **2h20min**).

Vers: the *lavoir* at the Place de la Fontaine (top) and the bell tower

Restaurants

If you visit *in summer,* you will have a good choice of places to eat, and our top recommendation would be the traditional restaurant at the Pont du Gard, **Les Terrasses**, on the right bank *(rive droite)* of the Gardon. Just look at the view from the terrace! This restaurant is open daily in summer and specialises in regional dishes; there are both set and à la carte menus. For more information see the website www.pontdugard.fr or (04 66 63 91 37. There's also a snack bar on the right bank called '**Le Bistrot**'.

But the best option, if you just want a light meal *all year round* (except Christmas Day) is to stay on the *rive gauche,* where there are three choices: a **café** serving hot and cold drinks, pastries and ice creams; '**Le Snack**', specialising in regional dishes and fresh produce like salads; and a **crêperie** with waffles as well as sweet and savoury crêpes (closed Nov/Dec).

Once back at Vers, the restaurant

Top: view from the terrace of the aptly-named Les Terrasses; above and below: 'Le Snack' — leafy in summer, cosy in the winter

restaurants

eat

La Petite Gare is nearby. This has now become the top restaurant in Vers with reviewers. We were last there two years ago, and enjoyed a superb meal: gazpacho to die for (with tomato sorbet on the side), steak tartare, and Thai red chicken curry. Your choice will be different: the menus change every two months. Look at the humorous website (in English) which will give you an idea of the imaginative dishes on offer as well as the lovely setting — cosy inside, but with a large garden under plane trees for warm days. There's a history, too, of the station — and a biography of the owner/chef.

La Petite Gare, at the old railway station just outside Vers

LA PETITE GARE
D192, 500m west of the Vers co-op
(04 90 95 58 43; lapetite gare.net   a l l year, Tue-Sat lunch and dinner €€-€€€

formule at 15 € (2 courses); other *formules* at 17 € and 29 €, with choices from the à la carte menu

menus at 20 € and 28 € (2 courses)

food to **take away**

Another of our favourite restaurants is at nearby Uzès: **L'Ecrin des Saveurs** (3, Boulevard Charles Gide, (04 66 22 35 21; no website, but look on Trip Advisor). Since they are not on the walking route, we didn't ply them with questions (or take a photo), but they seem to be open all day every day — there's never any problem getting a meal whenever we arrive! The choice is huge, and there are *menus* starting at 12 € for lunch (dish of the day and salad). It is the perfect restaurant for us, with simple meals like omelettes, pastas, pizzas, mussels and chips — *or* any Provençal speciality you can name. Full of local people all day long. Delicious, *if you have a car!*

Soupe au pistou (vegetable soup with *pistou*)

This Provençal speciality brings back fond memories. We were hoping to indulge again, but Le Provençal (see pages 130-131) was closed. We first had it there, many years ago, after walking over from Roussillon and climbing up to Gordes on a hot day in May. It was delicious — with a *bottle of red* wine. The plan had been to walk back, but below Gordes we found a shady tree and slept all afternoon…

In a large heavy saucepan, *gently stir-fry all the vegetables (except the peas and tomatoes)* in the oil, until soft but not browned. Pour over the stock, add the bouquet garni, and bring to the boil. Reduce the heat and simmer uncovered for 10 min. Add the peas and tomatoes and simmer for another 10 min. Now add the macaroni and tinned beans; simmer for 8-10 min, until the pasta is cooked.

Remove the bouquet garni, correct the seasoning, and serve in heated soup bowls garnished with the *pistou*.*

*If you are unable to find *pistou*, whizz together 50 g fresh basil leaves and a large clove of garlic. Add 1 skinned, de-seeded, chopped tomato and 30 g grated parmesan; blend again. *Gradually* add in 75 g olive oil, mixing until you have a fairly thick, pesto-like sauce.

Ingredients (for 4 servings)

1 potato, cut into chunks
1 yellow onion, thinly sliced
1 leek (including greens), sliced
1 carrot, sliced
50 g green beans, in pieces
1 courgette, coarsely chopped
50 g fresh or frozen peas
2 small tomatoes, skinned, de-
    seeded and diced
1.5 l chicken stock
1 cup tinned canellini beans
handful of macaroni
1 bouquet garni
2 tbsp olive oil
salt & pepper to taste
1 jar ready-made *pistou**

recipes

eat

One of our favourite hikes, this gorgeous, varied walk leads through dense *maquis*, with a huge variety of wild flowers, and a fairy-tale wood, before struggling up to a restored Saracen tower with panoramic views. The Tour des Opies, at 498m/1635ft, is the highest point in the Alpilles.

tour des opies
WALK

8

Start out at the **church** in **Aureille** (**O**). With your back to its door, turn left to a T-junction (with the boulangerie opposite). Head left on this main street, **Avenue Mistral**. Pass the **clock tower** on the right and, at the T-junction (**Place de la Fontaine**), turn right on the D25a (signposted to Les Baux and St-Rémy). You cross the river and very quickly come to the old **wash-house**, with Aureille's ruined castle rising above it. This is **Place du Lavoir**. Three narrow roads lead right out of this square; take the middle one, the **Rue du Lavoir** (**❶**). Follow this uphill, just at the right of and below the castle. At the **Place du Château** fork left, uphill — you can see Aureille's church over to the right. You're now on **Rue de la Savoie**; this becomes a cart track and runs above and to the left of the **cemetery**. At the far side of the cemetery, ignore a first gravel track off left (by a **shrine** on the left), but at the next track

Distance: 9.8km/6mi; 3h05min

Grade: moderate ascent of 350m/ 1150ft, but you must be sure-footed and agile. Do not attempt the summit on very windy days. Although the path is well used, be prepared to push through prickly broom. Little shade. GR waymarking at the start; variable waymarking to the pass; *none* to the summit. IGN map 3043 E

Equipment: see page 9; suitable clothing for dense undergrowth, walking stick(s), sun protection

Transport: 🚌 line 029 from **Arles** to Aureille (Arles—Salon line): departs *railway* station *(gare SNCF)* 08.38, 10.52 and 12.27 daily ex holidays; alight at Avenue de la Gare stop; journey time 50min. Returns at 16.49, 19.03 Mon-Sat, 20.23 daily ex holidays. Or 🚗 to Aureille

Refreshments: bar/café and restaurants at Aureille; nothing en route

Alternative walk: Strong walkers could combine this hike with Walk 9, allowing 20km/12.4mi; about 6h — a long and strenuous day out, with an overall ascent/descent of 450m/ 1475ft

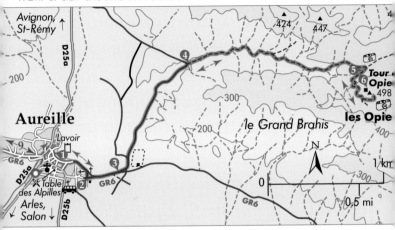

(almost immediately), turn left. There are two **GR signposts** here (**❷**; **7min**); follow the one for '**Eyguières, Lamanon**', ignoring the route to the right for Eygalières and Mouries. Your track heads due east through a barrier.

At a Y-fork after just 250m/yds, bear left, *leaving* the GR (**❸**; **15min**; there *may* be a **painted arrow** here). Follow this track, skirting just to the left of an **animal enclosure with trees**, being sure to ignore two tracks off to the left. Where your stony track bends hard left, 1km past the animal enclosure, fork right on a path (**❹**; **35min**). Be prepared now to push your way through shoulder-high thickets of prickly broom; the path itself is very clear underfoot. Keep right at a Y-fork (**55min**; **waymark** on a stone) and rise through the welcome shade of a dense woodland bower.

On reaching the **pass** below the tower (**❺**; **1h15min**; **huge** cairn), you enjoy a superb view north to the Vallon de Valdelègue; the tower is up to your right. From here take the path running sharply up to the right; it soon frays out into many strands (avoid minor short-cut paths to the left), but your goal is obvious. The path rounds the southwest side of the summit, comes to another

The flower-filled summit ascent path and the view from some rock pillars not far below the tower — to the flat summit of La Caume west of Aureille

huge **cairn**, then heads hard left. Just *before* reaching the **metal pole** below the tower, we find it easiest to turn up *right* for the final scramble.

From the **Tour des Opies** (**6**; **1h40min**) the views are tremendous, taking in Aureille far below, the Alpilles, La Caume with its transmitter, the Etang de Berre and

Mediterranean in the south, and — conditions permitting — Ste-Victoire to the east and even Mont Ventoux to the north!

Retrace your steps from here to the **cemetery** and

We took you the long way round to start the walk, to see the *lavoir* (above). Be sure to look around Aureille before you leave — there are lovely houses, the church and a separate clock tower.

follow the Rue de la Savoie uphill. Just past where the road becomes tarred, turn left down to the main road and make your way back to the **church** in the centre of **Aureille** (**O**; **3h05min**). La Table des Alpilles is in the **Place de l'Eglise**, if you've worked up an appetite!

La Table des Alpilles

This was our 'local' restaurant for years when checking nearby walks and arriving by car (there's good parking in the church square). It was a far simpler restaurant then, and we'd happily come in walking boots. But since 2015 it's been owned by a chef who trained at L'Oustau de Baumanière. We were a bit hesitant, but the staff are very accommodating to walkers — and in summer there's a terrace for outdoor dining.

Inside it's a real tonic on a winter's day when we tend to be here, bright and airy, with simply decorated and softly lit, rustic stone walls. And both the *formule* and the lower-priced *menu* are incredible value for such top-class food. He has no website, but there are plenty of photos of his dishes on the web.

LA TABLE DES ALPILLES
Place de l'Eglise (04 88 40 07 29
cl Mon, also Tue/Thu/Sun evenings
from Oct to Feb €€-€€€

lunch *formule* (Mon-Fri) at 18 €:
incredible value

otherwise *menus* at 20 € to 62 €

not an extensive menu, but then everything is seasonally and locally sourced and exquisitely presented

entrées like stuffed courgette flowers or shrimps in a pastry basket

mains might include *tatin* of lamb with aubergines or filet of St-Pierre in a sauce of citrus fruits and with a potato 'muffin' (John Dory, shown here)

desserts to die for — like chocolate delicacies or iced nougat with seasonal fruits…

restaurants

eat

Escalope de veau normande (veal escalope Normandy-style)

This is a dish we enjoyed at La Table's predecessor. Remember that veal escalopes are much thicker in France than those we are used to — they look more like pork. And this recipe works well with pork too.

First make the sauce. Gently cook the onion in butter until soft; then add the diced apple and cook for another 2 min. Shake over the flour and cook for 2 min more, stirring constantly, until thoroughly mixed. Add the cider and bring to the boil, still stirring. Season, and leave to simmer very gently for about 20 min while you make the garnish in a

separate pan: cook the sliced apple very gently until golden brown, then set aside and keep warm.

Lightly coat the meat in seasoned flour and fry for 2-5 min on each side (depending on thickness). Then remove from the pan and keep warm.

When the apple/onion has the consistency of apple sauce, add the cream and heat through, without letting it boil. Then pour through a strainer into the pan in which you cooked the meat, to take up its flavour. (At this stage we added some gravy browning to improve colour.) Spoon the sauce over the meat, and garnish with the apple slices.

Ingredients (for 4 people)

4 veal escalopes (or pork loin fillets)
1 medium onion, very finely chopped
2 large cooking apples, peeled and cored
— one very finely diced, the other finely sliced (to garnish)
500 ml dry cider
1 tbsp flour (from a shaker)
4 tbsp double cream
about 80 g butter
salt and freshly ground black pepper

Tapenade *(see photograph on page 77)*

Whizz together 250 g pitted black olives, 10 desalted, filleted anchovies, 50 g capers and black pepper to taste. Then, spoonful by spoonful, still mixing, add enough olive oil to make a pesto-like paste.

Moelleux au chocolat ('molten' chocolate)

This dessert often pops up on menus: it is a chocolate muffin-size cake with a liquid centre of melted ('molten') chocolate. Since it's made with flour (and the *authentic* version is very complicated), we've substituted our favourite 'molten' chocolate cake.

Preheat the oven to 190°C/375°F/ gas mark 5. Butter 4 ovenproof ramekins and keep ready on a baking tray.

Melt the chocolate in a flameproof bowl over simmering water (or melt it in a microwave). Then allow to cool slightly. Beat in the vanilla, sugar and brandy. Then add the egg yolks, one at a time, still beating. Finally, beat in the flour, until the mixture is stiff.

In a separate bowl, beat the egg whites until they form peaks, then gently fold them into the chocolate. Use a rubber spatula to ease the mixture into the ramekins, and bake for about 8-10 min, until well risen but still runny inside.

<u>Ingredients (for 4 people)</u>
150 g dark chocolate (minimum 70% cocoa solids), broken up
4 large eggs, separated
1 tbsp plain flour, sifted
85 g caster sugar
1/2 tsp vanilla
1 tbsp brandy
1 tsp butter

recipes

eat

Silvery leaves glisten beneath a porcelain-blue sky, and the air shimmers with heat, as you walk to the charming hamlet of Le Destet through olive groves typical of the Alpilles. Choose a cool day between October and May for this countryside ramble *in full sun*. At the end of the walk, Aureille is a welcoming place for a break or meal.

from aureille to le destet

WALK

Start out at the **church** in Aureille (**O**). With your back to its door, turn left to a T-junction (with the boulangerie opposite). Head left on this main street, **Avenue Mistral**. Pass the **clock tower** on the right and, at the T-junction (**Place de la Fontaine**), turn right on the D25a (signposted to Les Baux and St-Rémy). Then, at a junction after 60m/yds, turn left to cross the stream and follow **Chemin des Estendedous** (**①**), which is waymarked with red and white GR flashes.

Follow this to a Y-fork, where you keep right with the GR6 on the **Chemin de St-Jean**. Before long, the tar ends, and the GR turns up right (**②**). Keep ahead here, heading

Distance: 10.8km/6.7mi; 3h

Grade: easy, with ascents/descents of about 150m/490ft overall, but there is *no shade*. Some yellow local waymarking, some red and white GR waymarking. *IGN map 3043 E*

Equipment: see page 9; sun protection!

Transport: as Walk 8, page 109

Refreshments: bar/café and restaurants at Aureille; nothing en route (see page 113 for our suggestion)

Shorter walk: Vaudoret olive groves. 4.5km/2.8mi; 2h. Easy, with minimal ascents. Follow the main walk to the T-junction (**④**; 1h15min). Instead of turning left, head right, picking up the notes again at the 2h05min-point, to return to Aureille.

Alternative walk: Strong walkers could combine this hike with Walk 8, allowing 20km/12.4mi; 5h20min — a long and strenuous day out, with overall ascents/descents of about 500m/1640ft. Best suited to those travelling by car.

west. Under 10 minutes later you cross a **rushing watercourse**. Just beyond it, ignore a first track off left, but turn left on the next track, into the **Vaudoret olive groves** (**❸**; 30min).

Down in the heart of the groves, you meet a T-junction after 600m/yds: turn right into a quintessential Alpilles setting, with

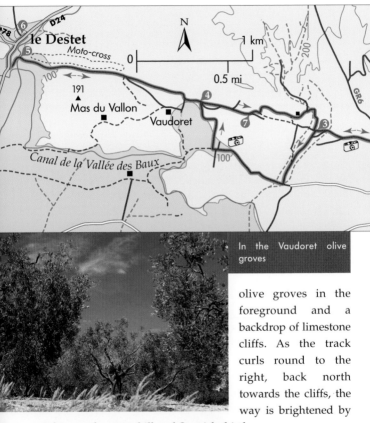

In the Vaudoret olive groves

olive groves in the foreground and a backdrop of limestone cliffs. As the track curls round to the right, back north towards the cliffs, the way is brightened by pinky-purple cranesbill and Scottish thistles.

After another 600m, ignore a cart track off right, then another off left a few paces further on. Ignore, too, a path

straight ahead after another 150m: bend 90°
right with the main track. When you come to a
T-junction (❹; **1h15min**), turn left. This track is a
continuation of the Chemin de St-Jean you took
from Aureille. Ignore two tracks off left to the
farm of Vaudoret (the first almost immediately,
the second ten minutes later). Soon you're
passing a **moto-cross circuit** on the right
(**1h25min**). Then you come to a lovely spot with
an **irrigation channel** (❺) on your left. On
meeting the **D24**, follow it to the right for about
300m/yds, just to see the lovely hamlet of **Le
Destet** (❻; **1h40min**).

Return the same way to the turn-off to the
moto-cross circuit. A sign here advertises biolo-
gical olive oil on sale at the Vaudoret *moulin* — a lovely
reminder of this walk, if you don't mind carrying it back to
Aureille! Continue trudging east along the track, past the moto-
cross, ignoring the tracks off right to the Vaudoret farm (unless
you want to visit and buy some oil). At the next, **three-way fork**
(❹; the T-junction at the 1h15min-point in the outward route;
now **2h05min**), you have a choice. You could turn right here
and retrace your route back through the olive groves — the
prettier route, but a bit longer.

For the main walk, take the middle track or the track on the
left (they rejoin). Four minutes later, ignore a track left uphill
but, three minutes/150m further on, at a **Y-fork** (❼), *do* go left
(and ignore a path off to the right a minute uphill). This track

The beautiful irrigation channel near Le Destet

skirts to the right of a cultivated field, then brushes up against the cliffs that border the northern edge of the route. Notice the turpentine trees, with their shiny leaves and autumn clusters of reddish-brown fruits.

You eventually approach a **smallholding** on the left (**2h 30min**). Continue past it on a cart track. It loops away from the cliff wall and skirts another field. A stream is on your right. Under four minutes (300m/yds) past the smallholding you're back at the point where you first turned down into the olive groves (**❸**).

Begin now to retrace your steps, first ignoring the track off right and then crossing back over the **rushing watercourse**. Keep ahead past another track off right, soon coming to a crest with a fine view ahead to Aureille, crowned by its château. A beautiful rounded mountain with a tower rises behind the village: Les Opies — the highest point in the Alpilles and goal of Walk 8.

On your return, just before forking right on Chemin des Estendedous, you could turn sharp right for 200m to this shrine, for a fine view towards the village and its ruined castle. From the bar/café at the end of the walk there's another lovely outlook — to the clock tower opposite, with the castle rising behind it.

Tar comes underfoot at the housing estate, and you rejoin the GR6. Continue along **Chemin des Estendedous**, turn right to recross the stream, and then go left to the **clock tower** in the centre of **Aureille** (**3h**). A bar/café is just opposite — or you could have a meal at La Table des Alpilles (see page 113) near the **church** (**O**), before going on to the bus stop.

121

The magnificent Abbaye de Sénanque, founded by Cistercian monks in the 12th century, is the goal of this walk. A wonderful feeling of tranquillity pervades the monastery, pure in line, and lacking in ornamentation. Gordes, a stunningly sited village, is another focal point, with much of interest and several good restaurants.

gordes and sénanque

WALK

10

Start the walk from the **bus stop** by the **fire/police station** (**O**) just outside **Gordes**. Continue along the D15 into the main square, the **Place du Château**, where the **Chapelle des Pénitents Blancs** is to your right. The **château** (with **tourist office**) is facing you; the entrance is on the far side of the building.

Facing our recommended restaurant, La Bastide de Pierres, and with the **château** *behind* you, ignore the D15 to Murs at the right of the restaurant, take the *next* road to the right, descending past the **post office** on your right. At a Y-fork, bear right, keeping the drystone walls of the **cemetery** (**1**) to your left. You may spot some faded waymarks on the wall here — and others further on — but don't rely on seeing them!

Beyond the cemetery gate (**5min**), the lane eventually

Distance: 10km/6.2mi; 3h

Grade: easy-moderate; ascents/descents of 300m/1000ft overall. The paths and tracks are fairly stony; little shade. No reliable waymarking to start, then red and white GR waymarking; IGN map 3142 OT

Equipment: see page 9

Transport: Transport by bus is daily *from mid-Apr to 1 Oct*, with a change at Cavaillon. 🚌 Line 7 from **Avignon** bus station *(gare routière)* at 08.50 daily, arrives **Cavaillon** 10.30. *Change to* 🚌 Line 17 to Gordes: departs 10.20; journey time 35min (total journey 2h). Or depart Avignon 12.15, arrive Cavaillon and take *connecting* Line 17 at 13.05 (journey time 1h25min). This latter bus runs Mon-Fri all year. Or 🚗 to Gordes. **Returns** from **Gordes** on 🚌 Line 17 to Cavaillon at 15.20 daily *from mid-Apr to 1 Oct*; arrives **Cavaillon** 15.50. *Change to* 🚌 Line 7 to Avignon: departs 16.15; journey time 45min. **No suitable return buses from 1 Oct to 15 Apr.**

Refreshments: Gordes

Shorter walk: to the Abbaye de Sénanque along the GR6 and back the same way — details on page 129.

Opening times/entry fee: see page 127

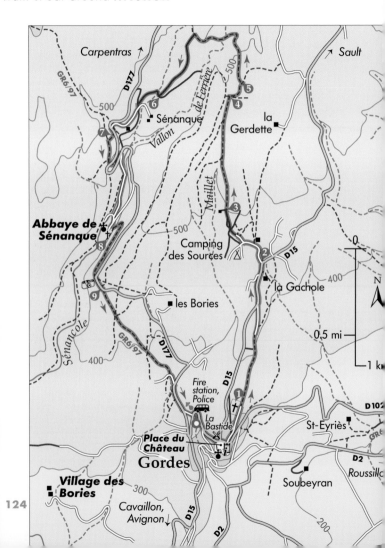

Carpentras

Sault

GR6/97

D177

de Ferrière

500

6

5

4

Sénanque

la Gerdette

7

Vallon

Maillet

3

Abbaye de Sénanque

500

Camping des Sources

2

D15

8

400

0

N

9

les Bories

la Gachole

Sénancole

GR6/97

D177

400

0,5 mi

1 k

Fire station, Police

D15

1

St-Eyriès

D102

GR6

Place du Château

La Bastide

Gordes

D2

Roussill

Village des Bories

Soubeyran

300

Cavaillon, Avignon ↓

D15

D2

200

loses its tarred surface. When you come onto tarmac again, by a house, keep straight ahead. Just past here, at a Y-fork, go left, with magnificent drystone walls on either side. Then meet the D15 and go straight ahead, until you can turn left uphill at a signpost for 'Camping des Sources' (**❷; 25min**). At the next fork, by the **campsite**, go left. You quickly come to some **letter boxes**, where you turn right on a tarmac lane. When the tarmac runs out, cross straight over a track and then keep right at a Y-fork. Soon

Some 3000 years of history unfold at the Village des Bories near Gordes, an outdoor museum of rural life. Bories are thought to date from the Bronze Age (while their exact origin is unknown, they resemble drystone dwellings as far afield as Ireland, Sardinia, the Balearics and Peru). Bories were inhabited until the 18th century.
There is an association in Vaucluse working for the preservation and restoration of drystone structures. One of their projects is especially fascinating: repairing the 12km-long 'Mur de la Peste', built in the 1720s between Monieux and Cabrières to halt the spread of the plague which was racing north from Marseille. At the height of the epidemic, 1000 soldiers manned this drystone wall.

the track turns off to the left (**❸**); take the path straight ahead here, heading due north, with fields to your right. The narrow path runs through *garrigues*; stunted oaks provide some shade. Clumps of tiny blue grass lilies dot the path, but only flower in May and June.

The picture-postcard view of Gordes — from the D15 (Cavaillon road)

Just over 1km further on, beyond more fields, you come to a T-junction (④; **1h05min**). There's a huge pine tree here, offering good shade for a break. Turn right but, after 150m/yds, go left **down a footpath** (⑤; various waymarks). This wide stony path descends into the **Vallon de Ferrière** — a basin of lavender cultivation. Cross the valley and then climb gently to the left of the lavender, ignoring the entrance to the farm on your right.

The **Sénancole Valley** opens up on the left now. Ignore a

track off left 150m/yds past the farm entrance but, at the next fork, just 50m further on, go left on a stony track and follow it southwest along the crest. Soon you have glimpses of the abbey, and you can see the Lubéron in the distance, rising from the plain.

When you meet the bend of a T-junction near the hamlet of **Sénanque** (⑥; **1h30min**), turn right downhill. The track curves left and into an open wood, another pleasant, shady spot. Five minutes later you reach a crossroads with several tracks.

Visiting Sénanque

While the surrounding grounds are freely accessible, the abbey itself (www.senanque.fr) can be visited on guided or unguided tours (7.50 €) from about 10.00-11.30 and 14.30-15.00 (depending on the season; see the website for detailed opening times). A guided tour is highly recommended, but note the comments at marvellous-provence.com — the best website we've seen for information: key in 'Senanque'. You must be modestly dressed for any visit. The monastery shop is open Mon-Sat 10.00-18.00 (Sun 14.00-18.00); closed most of Jan.

Keep straight ahead here on the level, motorable track. It passes to the right of a pecan grove and a large building (owned by the abbey), and takes you out to the D177 in five minutes. Cross the road and, 30m/yds downhill to the left, climb a path on the right (or if it is too overgrown and you don't see any faded waymarks after about 20 paces, keep to the road). In three minutes you meet a crossing path with red and white flashes (GR6/97): turn left downhill.

Follow the drive to the **Abbaye de Sénanque** (**1h50min**) and along the left side of the building. Just before a **statue of the Virgin Mary** (⑧), the GR turns off sharp left and then sharp

right, quickly gaining height and climbing to the D177 (**2h 10min**). Bear right on the road, to a sign, 'Côtes de Sénanque' (**9**). Just beyond here, turn right down a stony trail, from where you can see Gordes ahead. When you next meet the D177, follow it for 200m, then fork left down a lane. Meet the main road again, in **Gordes**, and turn left to the **bus stop** (**O**; **3h**).

Shorter walk: Gordes — Abbaye de Sénanque — Gordes.
6km/3.7mi; 2h30min. Grade as main walk (ascents/descents of about 250m/820ft overall). This walk follows the GR6 to the Abbaye de Sénanque and returns the same way. Although the GR starts just near the bus stop, we suggest that you first walk into the centre for lunch if you came by bus. Then **start out** from the main square. Facing La Bastide de Pierres (with the **château** behind you), walk back to the bus stop by following the **D15** signposted to Cavaillon and the abbey. Pass the **fire/police stations** and **bus stop** (**O**), and watch for a **fountain** with non-potable water on your right; turn sharp right uphill on a lane just past the fountain. Beyond a wooden gate on your right, you pick up a red and white GR waymark (five minutes from the château). On meeting the D177 go right but, after 200m, go left at a Y-fork (GR waymark). When you next meet the D177, bear left and follow it to a signpost, **Côtes de Sénanque** (**9**; viewpoint). Now continue ahead to another sign, '**garage 180m**', on your right. On your left a sign indicates a curve in the road: the path down left to the **Abbaye de Sénanque** (**8**) is just behind the sign. Retrace your route to back to the **bus stop** in **Gordes**.

Opposite: the Renaissance château at Gordes houses the tourist office

La Bastide de Pierres

For years our favourite place in Gordes was Le Provençal, right at the heart of things, with a lovely shady terrace and facing the château. It closed several years ago and stayed empty for years: a mystery, as it had *the best location* in town! But recently the property has been taken over by the 5-star hotel La Bastide: it's now an Italian restaurant and reviews are ecstatic. We've not been yet — can't wait to go! It's said to combine superb food with the chance to watch the world go by... and to our way of thinking, at least it will not be as here-today-gone-tomorrow as others in Gordes! It's fairly pricey; there must be a *menu* or *formule,* but it's not on their website.

LA BASTIDE DE PIERRES
Place du Château (04 90 72 18 91;
www.bastide-de-pierres.com
daily 12.15-15.00 and 19.15-22.15
€€-€€€

antipasti — of course — all kinds of Italian meats and cheeses, stuffed bell peppers, spring onions and baslamic vinegar

focaccie and bruschette salads (meals in themselves)

5 fresh **pastas** and 12 different wood-fired **pizzas**

3 quite elaborate **chef's specialities**: veal milanese with Italian cole slaw; beef carpaccio; fresh tuna in a pistacio crust with citrus salad and confit red onions ...

good selection of **Italian desserts and ice creams**

Veau marengo ('Napoleon's veal')

This veal dish was supposedly invented for Napoleon after his victory against Austria in the Battle of Marengo. It was the dish of the day at a super, tiny restaurant we found after Le Provençal closed. This 'find' is now *also* closed ('They set up, make their fortunes, and leave' a hard-working local grumbled.)

Heat 3 tbsp olive oil in a heavy-bottomed skillet and brown the meat on all sides. Add the shallots and garlic, and stir in just to soften. Then pour in the wine and bring to the boil. Lower the heat, add the tomato purée, stir, and leave to simmer, covered, for 2 h.

At this stage, it is better to cool the meat and finish the cooking the next day. Otherwise, sauté the mushrooms in 1 tbsp olive oil and, when soft, add to the meat mixture. Cover, and simmer again for 30 min. During this time, cook the tagliatelli (adding a tsp of olive oil to the water, to keep the pasta well separated).

Left: Behind the war memorial in Gordes is the Bastide de Pierres (ex Le Provençal; the photo was taken a couple of years ago), with shady terrace. L'Estaminet, shown at the far left, has acceptable food and welcoming staff, if La Bastide is full up.

Ingredients (for 4 people)

1 kg shoulder of veal, cut into large cubes
250 g tagliatelli
4 shallots, peeled and finely chopped
2 garlic cloves, peeled and finely chopped
400 g tin tomato purée
250 g mushrooms, sliced
250 ml dry white wine
4 tbsp olive oil
salt and freshly ground pepper

recipes

eat

Below are the websites where you can find more information about getting to Avignon by train and transport to and from the walks, as well as the villages or sites en route. Unfortunately, most of the transport information is only available in French — and often ambiguous. We cannot stress too strongly that it's best to get on-the-spot advice from the nearest tourist office or bus station: if you get stranded, taxis in this part of the world can be quite pricey (2.50-3.00 € per km) — especially if they have to come some distance to fetch you!

Avignon by train: Log on to **www.seat61** and search 'London to Avignon' for full details — this is an excellent website.

Walks 1, 2 and 3: While there *are* buses between Avignon, Nîmes and Arles, the fastest way of getting between these cities is by train. See page 12 for hints on using the website, **ter-sncf.com**. Otherwise, for buses, see the following sites:

> from Avignon: **www.edgard-transport.fr** *(English version)*;
> from Nîmes: **www.edgard-transport.fr** *(English version)*;
> from Arles: **www.tout-envia.com** *(English version)*.

The tourist office websites for these three cities all have English versions, sometimes with a link to public transport information:

> Avignon: **www.ot-avignon.fr**
> Nîmes: **www.ot-nimes.fr**
> Arles: **www.arlestourisme.com**

Walk 4: The easiest way to get bus timetables for St-Rémy (and Les Baux!) is to go to the town's official website, **www.saintremy-de-provence.com** and, in the English version, click on 'Informations', then 'St-Rémy access'; there are bus timetables to download.

WEB SITES

Walk 5: Les Baux's website is **www.lesbauxdeprovence.com**, but there are no timetables. St-Rémy's website (see Walk 4 above) includes the timetable for Les Baux (Avignon–Arles line).

Walk 6: Barbentane is served by bus line 56 (Avignon–Tarascon line); timetables at **www.le pilote.com** (site in French: select 'Horaires' and key '56' at 'Numéro ou nom de la ligne'). The Barbentane tourist office can be accessed at **www.barbentane.fr** (site only in French).

Walk 7: Timetables for bus lines B21 (Nîmes–Pont St-Esprit) and A15 (Avignon–Alès) can both be found at **www.edgard-transport.fr**; the Vers tourist office site can be accessed at **www.vers-pont-du-gard.fr** (for English text, click on 'Traductions' under 'Vie pratique', then 'en anglais'); another website, **ot-pontdugard.com** (in English) has information about all the villages in the area; the official website for the Pont du Gard complex itself (with all its amenities) is at **www.pontdugard.fr** (of course in English too).

Walk 8 and 9: Timetables for bus line 029 (Arles–Salon route) can be downloaded at **www.lepilote.com** (site in French: select 'Horaires' and key '029' at 'Numéro ou nom de la ligne'). The website for Aureille village is at **aureille.fr** (site only in French).

Walk 10: Getting to Gordes means two buses, but timings are very convenient from mid-April to October 1st, when buses run daily. The entire journey only takes about 1h10min, including the change of buses at Cavaillon bus station (the timetables are synchronised). Go to **luberoncotesud.com** (only in French) and at the search box key in 'horaires de bus'. This brings up a page where you can download timetables for Transvaucluse bus Line 7 (Avignon–Cavaillon) and Line 17 (Cavaillon–Gordes–Apt). The website for the Gordes Tourist Office is **www.gordes-village.com** (with English version), but it has no information on public transport. The website for the Abbaye de Sénanque is **www.senanque.fr** (in French, but with some very brief explanations in English).

We've been exploring Provence for many years, doing what we like most — walking, eating and sampling local wines. Before we started our own publishing company and had more leisure time (and money!), our excursions were often based on the many châteaux-hotels in the area. We toured from place to place, stayed a night or two, with a good hike during the day and a 5-star meal in the evening.

In the late 1990s John had to get to grips with the first of his food intolerances, when he was diagnosed coeliac (no more *baguettes* for the lunchtime picnic during a hike, no more *croissants* with 'elevenses', no more *tarte aux pommes*)!

Some coeliacs become lactose intolerant over time; many other people are lactose intolerant without being coeliac. True lactose intolerance doesn't just mean avoiding cow's milk, etc, but *all* milks, butters, creams, yoghurts, and cheeses — whether from cows, goats or sheep. Another blow — no more *fromage…*

Food intolerances are becoming ever more common, and we know *there are a lot of you out there!* Even if you have learned to cope at home, it can be very daunting to go on holiday. *Will the food in restaurants be safe? Will I be able to buy gluten- and dairy-free foods?*

If you suffer a food intolerance you have probably already learned at home that what initially seems a penance in fact becomes a challenge and eventually a joy. We eat far healthier meals now than we did before, with fewer additives.

EAT GF, DF

Nowhere is this more enjoyable than in Provence, where olive oil, fish, tomatoes and 'alternative' grains and flours are basic to the diet. Many, many dishes are *naturally* gluten- and dairy-free.

Of course food intolerances *are* restrictive — in the sense that we have to carry, buy or bake gluten-free breads and sweets, and we always need access to dairy-free 'milk', 'cream', 'yoghurt' and 'butter'. So over the years we've sussed out eating gf, df around the area, and it's *so simple*.

EATING IN RESTAURANTS

Many **entrées** are suitable, among them cold meat plates or marinated vegetables. Bring your own bread! Salads are also common, just avoid those with cheese. The ubiquitous brown fish soup (*soupe de poissons;* also sold in supermarkets) is also gf, df — just bring your own gf croutons.

For **main courses** one is spoilt for choice. If you're a sauce addict, like John, here's some very good news. Sauces are virtually *always* made by 'reduction' (cooked over a moderate heat until it becomes syrupy, as opposed to being thickened with wheat flour). But of course, you will *ask in advance* (see inside back cover). Many **steaks** are served in a mushroom and wine sauce — or with *foie gras.*

Anything '*à la provençale*' will be gf, df — generally this means with tomato, onion and garlic, as well as other spices and perhaps mushrooms, black olives and/or anchovies.

Fish dishes, unless grilled or poached, *may* well contain a least a dusting of wheat flour, since fish is quite difficult to fry otherwise. *But not impossible.* If you ask, in a restaurant that *you trust*, they will do it without flour (or bring your own flour). Ask also if the sauce contains any cream or milk.

Give the **cheese course** a miss — unless, like John, you break out the 'lactase tablets' (now widely available at chemists and health food shops; just search the web) and treat yourself for a change. They really do work, and he uses them for special occasions (a magnificent cheese board) or for a 'full works' omelette (it is so much better with cheese) or for *moules farcies* in butter.

We are usually too full to have **dessert**, which is just as well, since virtually all the sweet courses in the restaurants we recommend contained flour and/or cream or ice cream. If you have a sweet tooth, make for Aux Porte Mages in Les Baux, there are many exotic sorbets — with or without liqueur! Otherwise, almost all the restaurants can offer seasonal fruit.

SELF-CATERING

While many hotels cater for food intolerances, we discovered the joy of self-catering — whether in a country cottage or an apart-hotel in the city — years ago. What a liberation! Room to swing a cat (or, more likely, chop up a rabbit). Tables where you can spread out your maps and bus timetables. Sofas to loll about on with a good book on a rainy day.

But for a special occasion, we might just book a night or two in one of the châteaux for old time's sake; it's relatively easy to cope for just a couple of nights. Then back to base with the laundry and gf bread waiting in the freezer.

Gf, df shopping

From a niche market when we wrote the first edition of this book, catering for food intolerances has grown 10-fold in France — almost as much as it has in the UK.

Valpiform is one of the French market leaders in gf products, but **Gerblé** and **Schär** (Italian) are also popular and are usually sold in Monoprix, Casino, Leclerc, Auchan, SuperU and Carrefour markets, all of which have 'free-from' sections. In all **Monoprix** supermarkets (see our town plans) this area is usually called '**Produits biodiététiques**'.

If the dairy-free products are not with the gf selection, just ask for 'soja' — there has always been a good selection of soya milks and sweets in France; the milk may be kept with the UHT milk, the sweets in the chill cabinet.

GF, DF supermarket shopping

The large supermarket chains stock some very useful products (but not always in their mini-markets):

Tournolive is top of our list — a dairy-free cooking/baking/spreading margarine, which tastes delicious and does *not* spit when used for frying;

soya milk and yoghurts — natural or flavoured — which can be bought in small containers;

Camargue salt *(fleur de sel)*; this usually comes in such a lovely container with cork lid that it makes a great and inexpensive gift for those back home;

jams (Baptistin Feraud is particularly good);

gf, df tinned 'stews': Look out for *Saucisses aux lentilles* and *Petit salé aux lentilles*. Mix either with a tin of chopped tomatoes and a glass of wine and *voilà*: dinner in a moment! (*Beware*: not all brands of these tinned stews are gf, so read the label; Jardin Bio is usually fine)

soupe de poissons: this comes in a large glass jar (either in the chiller or shelved with other soups), and all those we have seen are gf, df.

If you cannot find all you need in the supermarket, try these *central** health food shops (shown on the plans):

Avignon

- **Le Panier des Amis**, Les Halles (℘ 04 90 87 14 32)
- **Naturalia**, 54 Rue de la Bonneterie (℘ 09 64 45 80 38)

Nîmes

- **BioBoutique**, 28b Rue Notre Dame (℘ 04 66 64 60 22)

Some of the things to look out for in specialist shops are:

- simply delicious soya yoghurts. There is a great variety available in small sizes (150 g), in both glass jars and plastic containers;
- soya, almond or rice 'milks', such as Provamel Bio Soya;
- soya 'cream' — a *must* for cooking. In France it is called Provamel Soya *Cuisine* (it's the same product that is available in the UK as Provamel Soya *Dream*);
- gluten-free breads: a great chance to try different national offerings: French Valpiform and Pleniday, Italian Schär (some of our favourites) and Glutano, as well as Spanish Procelli (lovely croissants);
- Barilla is the up-and-coming brand for pastas
- gluten-free biscuits: Schär has both sweet and plain, and their biscuits for cheese are superb;
- gluten-free flour: all kinds of flours are on sale;
- Rapunzel 'Soma' dairy-free margarine made in Avignon; contains 50% sunflower oil and *doesn't spit* when frying.

*If you have a car or are willing to take a taxi (7-8km from Avignon central station) to the Avignon Nord Commercial Centre, it would be worth stocking up at the large **Pleine Nature** (℘ 04 90 32 65 33), which also has a restaurant.

Gf, df cooking

We've made all the **recipes** in this book using gluten- and dairy-free ingredients. Basically we just used a 1:1 substitution — remember, we are just amateur cooks — and the cooking method

'Salade gourmande' at Le Romarin in Barbentane (see page 96)

was unchanged. We've been more than happy with the results! The only problem we have is *frying* — but never in France. All the margarines we buy in England contain a lot of water and spit all over the place. But Tournolive (from supermarkets) and Soma (from health food shops) are a dream to use.

CONVERSION TABLES

Weights		Volume		Oven temperatures		
						gas
10 g	1/2 oz	15 ml	1 tbsp	°C	°F	mark
25 g	1 oz	55 ml	2 fl oz			
50 g	2 oz	75 ml	3 fl oz	140°C	275°F	1
110 g	4 oz	150 ml	1/4 pt	150°C	300°F	2
200 g	7 oz	275 ml	1/2 pt	170°C	325°F	3
350 g	12 oz	570 ml	1 pt	180°C	350°F	4
450 g	1 lb	1 l	1-3/4 pt	190°C	375°F	5
700 g	1 lb 8 oz	1.5 l	2-1/2 pt	200°C	400°F	6
900 g	2 lb			220°C	425°F	7
1.35 g	3 lb			230°C	430°F	8
				240°C	475°F	9

MENU ITEMS

à point medium rare
agneau lamb
aigre-doux sweet and sour
ail garlic
aïoli garlic mayonnaise (also salt cod, hard-cooked eggs, boiled snails, and vegetables served with garlic mayonnaise; specialty of Provence)
aiglefin haddock
aiguillette long thin slice
amande almond
amer bitter
anchoïade sauce of anchovies, olive oil and garlic
anchois anchovy
andouille smoked tripe sausage
andouillette small tripe sausage
aneth dill
anis aniseed
arachide peanut
arête fish bone (*sans arêtes =* filleted)
aromates aromatic spices

artichaut artichoke
asperges asparagus
assiette de plate of
avocat avocado
basilic basil
bleu very rare
blettes Swiss chard
boeuf beef
bourride fish stew
brandade de morue salt cod
brochette skewered
cabillaud fresh cod
caille quail
calamars squid
canard duck
caneton duckling
cannelle cinnamon
carré cutlet or chop from best end of neck
carvi caraway
céléri celery
céléri-rave celeriac
cèpes large, meaty wild mushrooms
champignons mushrooms
 de paris button — button
chanterelles golden-coloured wild mushrooms
chèvre goat (cheese)
chevreau kid
choix, au choice of
chou cabbage

choucroute sauerkraut; also dish of sauerkraut, pork and sausages (or seafood!), served with potatoes
chou-fleur cauliflower
cochon de lait suckling pig
coco blanc small white shell bean
confit preserved
coquillages shellfish
coquilles st-jacques scallops
côte chop, side
coulis thick sauce
courge pumpkin
crabe crab
crevettes
 grises shrimp
 roses prawns
crudités raw vegetables
daube stew
daurade/dorade sea-bream
dinde/dindon turkey
écrevisses freshwater crayfish
entrecôte rib steak
escabèche marinated fish or poultry, served cold
escargots snails

espadon (Mediterranean) swordfish
estouffade beef stew with onions, herbs, red wine
faisan pheasant
feuilletée puff pastry
foie liver
foie gras goose liver
fricandeau slice of topside veal
fritures tiny fried fish
fruits de mer seafood
galette de sarrasin buckwheat crêpe (see page 77)
gambas giant prawns
gesiers gizards
gibier game
gratiné browned (often with butter and breadcrumbs)
grenadin thick veal escalope
grenouille frog
 cuisse de — frogs' legs
grillé grilled
farci stuffed
faux-filet sirloin
haricots beans
 — verts green beans

GLOSSARY

homard lobster
huîtres oysters
jambon ham
  fumé smoked
jarret knuckle
langouste spiny lobster
lapin rabbit
lardons bacon bits
légumes vegetables
longue loin
lotte (de mer) monkfish
loup (de mer) sea-bass
magret de canard breast of fattened duck
merguez spicy sausage
miel honey
mignon small (round) piece
mijoté simmered
moelleux 'molten' (see page 115)
morilles wild morel mushrooms
morue salt cod
moules mussels
noisette small round piece
noix nuts
oignon onion
pain bread
pâtes pasta
pané with bread-crumbs
papillote parchment paper or foil wrapping

paupiette slice of meat or fish, filled, rolled and wrapped up
pavé thick slice
pêche peach
persil parsley
persillade chopped parsley and garlic
petit small
pieds et paquets mutton tripe with sheep's feet, white wine, and tomatoes (speciality of Provence)
pignons pine nuts
pistou mixture of garlic, basil, tomatoes, parmesan and olive oil (see page 107)
poêlé pan-fried
poire pear
poireau leek
poisson fish
poivron sweet pepper
pomme apple
pommes de terre potatoes
pot-au-feu beef simmered with vegetables
Provençale, à la with tomatoes, olive oil, garlic
raie skate
raisins grapes
rascasse scorpion fish

ravigote sauce with onions, herbs, mushrooms, wine vinegar
rémoulade sauce with mayonnaise, mustard, capers, anchovies, herbs
rognons kidneys
Rossini with foie gras
roti roast
rouget red mullet
rouille mayonnaise-like sauce with peppers, garlic and saffron
safran saffron
sanglier wild boar
sandre perch-like fish
saumon salmon
sole sole
souris lamb shank
suprême boneless breast
tapenade paste of black olives, anchovies and capers (called 'Provençal caviar')
tarte open pastry case
taureau bull
telline small clam
terrine cold 'loaf' of fish, meat or pâté (named for the container in which it is cooked)
tourte sweet-filled pastry case, pie

truccha Avignon-style omelette with Swiss chard or wild asparagus and garlic
turbot/turbotin turbot
velouté white sauce
veau veal
volaille poultry

SHOPPING TERMS

anchovies *anchois*
apple *pomme*
artichoke *artichaut*
asparagus *asperges*
avocado *avocat*
bacon bits *(lardons)*
  unsmoked *(lardons nature)*
bass, sea *loup de mer*
bay leaf *laurier*
beans *haricots*
  green *haricots verts*
beef *boeuf* cuts:
  boneless *sans os*
  fillet *filet*
  fore rib *entrecôte*
  rib *côte*
  rump *rumsteak*
  shin *jarret*
  shoulder *paleron*
  sirloin *faux-filet*
beer *bière*
blackberries *mûres*
brandy *cognac*
bread *pain*
bream, sea *daurade*

butter *beurre*
cake *gâteau*
carrot *carotte*
celeriac *céléri-rave*
celery *céleri*
chard, Swiss *blettes*
cheese *fromage*
cherries *cerises*
chicken *poulet*
chocolate *chocolat*
cider *cidre*
cloves *girofles*
cod (salt) *morue;*
 (fresh) *cabillaud*
coffee *café*
condiments *condi-*
 ments
corn
 meal *farine de*
 maïs
 starch *amidon de*
 maïs
courgettes *cour-*
 gettes
crab *crabe*
crayfish *écrevisses*
cream *crème*
cucumber
 concombre
duck *canard*
 preserved *confit*
eggs *oeufs*
fennel *fenouil*
fish *poisson*
flour (wheat) *farine*
fruit *fruit*
game *gibier*
garlic *ail*
goose *oie*
 grease *graisse*
 d'oie

goose liver *foie gras*
grapes *raisins*
haddock *aiglefin*
ham *jambon*
 smoked *fumé*
herbs *herbes*
ice cream *glace*
juice *jus*
juniper *genièvre*
lamb agneau
 cuts:
 boneless *sans os*
 cutlets from best
 end of neck *carré*
 leg (including
 chump) *gigot*
 loin *filet*
 shank *souris*
 shouler *épaule*
leek *poireau*
lemon *citron*
lettuce *laitue*
liver *foie*
lobster *homard*
 spiny *langouste*
milk *lait*
monkfish *lotte de*
 mer
mullet, red *rouget*
mushrooms *cham-*
 pignons
mussels *moules*
mustard *moutarde*
nuts *noix*
 peanuts *arachides*
olive oil *huile d'olive*
onions *oignons*
oysters *huîtres*
parsley *persil*
pasta *pâtes*
pastry *pâtisserie*

pear *poire*
peas *pois/petits pois*
pepper (spice)
 poivre
pepper (sweet)
 poivron
pheasant *faisan*
pine nuts *pignons*
pork porc
 rind *couennes*
 cuts:
 boneless *sans os*
 chop *côte*
 cutlet from best
 end of neck *carré*
 escalope *escalope*
 fillet *filet*
 loin *longue*
potatoes *pommes*
 de terre
poultry *volaille*
prawns *crevettes*
 giant *gambas*
pumpkin *courge*
quail *caille*
rabbit *lapin*
raspberries
 framboises
rice *riz*
rosemary *romarin*
saffron *safran*
salmon *saumon*
salt *sel*
 sea *(fleur de sel)*
sausage
 fresh *saucisse*
 dry *saucisson*
scallops *coquilles*
 (St-Jacques)
shallots *echalotes*
shellfish *coquillages*

shrimp *crevettes*
 grises
snails *escargots*
sole *sole*
soup *soupe*
soya *soja*
spices *épices*
spinach *épinards*
sugar *sucre*
tarragon *estragon*
tea *thé*
thyme *thym*
tomatoes *tomates*
tuna *thun*
turbot *turbot,*
 turbotin
turkey *dindon*
 young *dinde*
veal veau
 cuts:
 boneless *sans os*
 chop *côte*
 fillet *filet*
 kidneys *rognons*
 liver *foie*
 loin *carré*
 shin, knuckle *jarret*
 shoulder *épaule*
 sweetbreads *ris*
 topside *noix*
vegetables *légumes*
vinegar *vinaigre*
wine de *vin*
water *eau*
 still *sans gaz*
 sparkling *avec gaz*
watercress *cresson*
wine *vin*
 dry *sec*
 red *rouge*
 white *blanc*

bold type: photograph; *italic type:* map

INDEX

Third edition © 2019
Published by Sunflower Books
PO Box 36061, London SW7 3WS
www.sunflowerbooks.co.uk

ISBN 978-1-85691-515-1

Cover photograph: Pont St-Bénézet and the St-Nicolas chapel

Photographs: John Underwood except for the cover (Shutterstock)
Maps: Sunflower Books
Cookery editor: Marina Bayliss
Series designed by Jocelyn Lucas
A CIP catalogue record for this book is available from the British Library.
Printed and bound in England by Short Run Press, Exeter

Before you go ...
log on to
www.sunflowerbooks.co.uk
and click on the 'Provence' page, then on '**updates**', to see if we have been notified of any changes to the routes or restaurants.

When you return ...
do let us know if any routes have changed because of council re-routing, new waymarking, storm damage or the like. Have any of our restaurants closed? Feel free to suggest other restaurants for the on-line update, but please bear in mind that these books are not intended to be complete restaurant guides!
Send your comments to info@sunflowerbooks.co.uk